The Story of
Mount Desert Island, Maine

BOOKS BY SAMUEL ELIOT MORISON

THE STORY OF
Mount Desert Island
MAINE

by

SAMUEL ELIOT MORISON

WITH ILLUSTRATIONS

An Atlantic Monthly Press Book

BOSTON · Little, Brown and Company · TORONTO

FIRST EDITION

F
27
M9
M6

ATLANTIC–LITTLE, BROWN BOOKS
ARE PUBLISHED BY
LITTLE, BROWN AND COMPANY
IN ASSOCIATION WITH
THE ATLANTIC MONTHLY PRESS

Published simultaneously in Canada
by Little, Brown & Company (Canada) Limited

41766

PRINTED IN THE UNITED STATES OF AMERICA

To my Dearest Wife
Priscilla Barton Morison
who beautifully provided the song
to our "Evening of Song and Story"
29 July 1959

Foreword

IN 1961 the permanent settlement of Mount Desert Island will be two centuries old, and the Island has passed through many phases before becoming the nucleus of the Acadia National Park. Prior to the settlement, there are stories of Champlain's discovery and naming of the Island in 1604, of Madame de Guercheville's short-lived mission, and the grant to the self-styled Sieur de Cadillac. And behind the first visits of Europeans, archaeologists have found records of occupation by Indians for about five thousand years.

These rather random notes have been gathered over the many years that I have enjoyed summers at Northeast Harbor. They were put together for an informal lecture that I gave, in conjunction with a song recital by my wife Priscilla Morison, for the benefit of the Island libraries, in July 1959. Other data have been added, in order to make a permanent record.

I wish to express gratitude for help given to me by Mrs. Stella Hill, Mrs. Belle Smallidge Knowles, Mrs. John Pelz, Mrs. W. Rodman Fay, Mrs. Roy Pier, Colonel Frank B. Alley, Mrs. Harold Peabody, Dr. Wendell S. Hadlock, Mr. Charles Savage, Mr. Paul G. Favour of the National Park Service, Mr. Herman R. Friis of the National Archives, and Dr. K. Jack Bauer of Washington. Many others, too, have lent me photographs to be used as illustrations, or told me facts and anecdotes.

This has indeed been a "labor of love" for the people and the place, the beloved Island of Mount Desert.

S. E. Morison

"Good Hope"
Northeast Harbor
October, 1959

Contents

Illustrations

(Illustrations appear between pages 36 and 37)

The Story of
Mount Desert Island, Maine

1. The Indians

IT is only four hundred years since the first European saw the hills of Mount Desert arise like blue bubbles from the sea; but the Indians had already been using its shores and waters for several thousand years. Three different Indian cultures have occupied its territory. Archaeologists have discovered a cache of Indian relics, edged tools, spearheads, and slate lance-points near Ellsworth Falls, which by the Carbon-14 method of dating must have been deposited around 4000 B.C., and which resemble objects found in New Mexico and Arizona more than those turned up elsewhere in New England. Among the artifacts are found the bones of the tuna fish. Since the tuna never enters bays and harbors if he can help it, these early inhabitants of Ellsworth must have pursued the big game fish in their canoes as far south as Bakers and the Duck Islands; certainly outside Blue Hill Bay and Frenchmans Bay.

The tuna fishermen, around 1000 A.D., were replaced by, or developed into, the Indians who for want of a better term are called the Red Paint People, because they were highly addicted to make-up. In their graves are found caches of red and yellow ochre with which they adorned their faces and bodies. Red Paint relics, found at Blue Hill, Hancock Point and Ellsworth, are similar to those of the so-called Mound Builders of the Middle West. These people made cutting tools of slate, fashioned pottery, and used iron pyrites to strike a fire with flint; but they knew not the use of tobacco.

Whence came the Red Paint People, why they left or were replaced, we simply do not know — perhaps they were too busy with their make-up to defend themselves. They may have been early Algonkin or Abnaki, who developed the birch-bark culture that we associate with the Indians of historic times; or they may have been conquered by the Indians whom the earliest Europeans encountered.

These were Abnaki, who belonged to the Algonkian language group, one of the most important branches of American Indians, at one time covering most of Eastern United States and Canada. The Penobscot and Passamaquoddy tribes of the Abnaki were the Indians encountered at Mount Desert by the first Europeans. They were tobacco smokers, potters, and remarkable craftsmen with birch bark — they could even make a birch-bark bucket in which you could boil water.

The Abnaki Indians were not permanent residents of Mount Desert; only summer folk — like some of us. Their permanent villages were up the Penobscot near Orono and on the headwaters of the Machias and Narraguagus Rivers. In the spring they planted beans and corn at their villages, and left behind the old people to tend them and scare off deer and crows. Then each family — braves, squaws, children, papooses and dogs — piled into birch-bark canoes and made for Pemetic, their name for Mount Desert Island. For those who did not care to risk the rough water off Bass Harbor or Great Head, there is an inside canoe route, which I have taken, myself — from Goosemarsh Harbor via Round Pond, Great Pond, Ripple Pond and Somes Pond — leading from upper Blue Hill Bay into Somes Sound.

At various points on Frenchmans Bay and the shores of Mount Desert, but always near tidal flats where the clam flourished, they set up their birch-bark lodges for the summer season. While the men went fishing or lay about smoking pipes and telling tall tales, the squaws dug clams, which they shucked out and hung on spruce roots stretched from tree to tree so that the dogs couldn't get at them, though the flies did (but the Indians didn't mind flies). The squaws also gathered sweet grass and peeled birch bark to make their baskets and boxes. The children played and picked wild berries; the young people made love. All waxed fat and happy during the summer months at Pemetic. In early October, when the trees began to turn, the squaws packed their dried clams and berries and smoked fish into bark boxes, loaded the family canoe, and all returned to the home village to greet Grandpa and Grandma and to harvest the corn crop. During the winter the women, children and old men stayed at home while the young men and big boys went hunting on snowshoes for deer and moose, and set traps for the beaver from whose pelts they made most of their clothes. Sometimes they returned to the Island to hunt moose, for which Pemetic was noted. By chasing the moose with lighted torches they drove them into the water where they could be killed, while swimming, with bow and arrow.

This was a good life that the Europeans disturbed, then broke up. It went on for hundreds of years, as the deep shell-heaps on Frenchmans Bay, at Northeast Harbor, and on Fernalds Point prove. And as Chief Asticou, the Sagamore of Kenduskeag, located at the entrance of Somes Sound, we may call Manchester Point the summer capital of the Penobscot tribe.

When the English began to settle, the Indians gradually broke off this seasonal visiting. But some of them still came to camp on the shores of Somes Pond, to fish and to trap mink. Mrs. Adelma F. Joy, who remembered them there around 1840, wrote a charming poem about these summer encampments:

I loved the Indian, when he built his wigwam by the pond
And hunted, unmolested. No canvas wigwam had he,
But one of boughs. I've sat and watched the squaws
Doing their beadwork, and wished I were an Indian.

They were our friends, and we were theirs;
They came and we welcomed them: they lived upon our land,
No rent was paid or asked, our children played with theirs.

They often made us visits, wearing their bright plaid shawls
And shining beaver hats. They sat at table with them on;
It was their custom. We treated them like honored guests,
And they looked it. Why should we not?
Were they not here before us?

2. The European Discovery

WHO was the first European to see Mount Desert Island? This question can never be answered certainly. The imaginative Mr. Frederick J. Pohl brings the Northmen here; but there is no concrete evidence of it, and much to indicate that the Northmen came no farther south than Newfoundland. Credulous people are said to be searching here with geiger counters for the grave of Leif Ericson, which will give them plenty of exercise and do no harm. John and Sebastian Cabot may well have come this way, because the Cabots get around — our John has gone to Rio where a certain distinguished lady was not allowed to go! But the first European whom we positively know saw Mount Desert Island was Estévan Gomes (i.e., Stephen Smith), a Portuguese in the Spanish service who was sent on a voyage along this coast in 1525 with orders to find a strait leading to the Pacific — a northern Panama. When he hit the Penobscot River, which he called *Rio de las Gamas* (River of the Deer), Steve thought he had it and sailed up to the site of Bangor, where he decided he hadn't; but he observed that the Indians were using the islands in Penobscot Bay as summer resorts, and some of them he kidnaped and sold in Spain. Steve's explorations are recorded on a world map by Diego Ribero, another Portuguese, in 1529; and this map was copied and recopied for almost a hundred years, until Champlain made a better one.

On Ribero's map you find, between *Rio de las Gamas* and the Bay of Fundy, a *Rio de Montanas*, River of Mountains. Since the only river or estuary east of the Penobscot which has mountains on each side is Somes Sound, Mount Desert, it is obvious that that is what Steve saw in 1525. The map, to be sure, does not show *Rio de Montanas* to be on an island; but nobody sailing along the coast and not exploring the two bays up to the Narrows would have known that Mount Desert was an island. Even the English *Coast Pilot* of 1739 shows our mountains on the mainland, strung along Eggemoggin Reach.

We now skip eighty years to the voyages of the great Samuel de Champlain, father of New France. Champlain came out in 1604 as pilot, guide, and general handyman to the Sieur de Monts, who had a grant from Henri IV, King of France, to *La Cadie* (*L'Acadie*, or Acadia) which has given the name to our National Park. La Cadie, the French version for an Indian name meaning "The Place," comprised the entire French claim to North America from latitude 40° (Philadelphia) to latitude 46° (Montreal). De Monts had a wide choice for locating his first trading post and colony, but he picked out perhaps the most unsuitable site in the entire area — a little island in the St. Croix River, later called Dochet, and now the St. Croix National Park. Once established there, De Monts sent Champlain in the smallest of his vessels, a *patache* — a square-rigged ketch of 17 tons — to explore the coast of L'Acadie and look for "Norumbega." That was a mythical walled and wealthy city on the Penobscot, built entirely out of fancy by the Indians in their talks with the French — partly because they liked to please, and partly because they liked telling tall tales.

In September 1604 Champlain, with twelve sailors and

two Indian guides, cleared Quoddy Narrows and sailed along the Maine coast. He rounded and named Petit Manan, spent a night somewhere on the east side of Schoodic Point, and, on the 6th, crossed Frenchmans Bay. Attracted by smoke arising from an Indian encampment on Otter Creek, he steered for Otter Cliff and, at high water with a smooth sea, hit the ledge off that point, which is now marked by a bell buoy. "This island," wrote Champlain, "is very high, and cleft into seven or eight mountains, all in a line. The summits of most of them are bare of trees, nothing but rock. I named it l'Isle des Monts-déserts" (i.e., the Isle of Bare Mountains).[1] After repairing the hole in his *patache* at Otter Creek, where he picked up two friendly Indians as guides, Champlain either sailed up Frenchmans Bay to ascertain that Mount Desert was indeed an island, or, as is more likely, took the Indians' word for it. At any rate, he states correctly

[1] His exact words are: "*Le sommet de la plus part d'icelles est desgarny d'arbres parceque ce ne sont que roches. Je l'ay nommée l'Isle des Monts-déserts.*" Right here we may grapple with the problem how to pronounce it in English — whether we should follow what many people call the "Sahara School" and accent the penult, pronouncing it "Mount Dez'-ert," or what opponents call the "Ice Cream and Cake School," pronouncing it "Mount Dez-ert'" with accent on the last syllable. I should say that the spelling "Mount Desart" on *The Atlantic Neptune* and other old maps indicates that, like "clerk," "sergeant," and other words containing "er," it was pronounced "ar," and that the accent was then on the last syllable. Charles Tracy recorded, in his journal of 1855, that the natives called it Mount Desert'," Lippincott's *Pronouncing Gazetteer*, edition of 1883, says "dez-ert' or dez-art'." During my youth most of the older inhabitants called it "Mount Dez'-ert" (although inconsistently they called the steamboat of that name the *Mount Dez-ert'*), and President Eliot pronounced in favor of the Sahara School. Bishop Doane, on the other hand, unwilling to take orders from a Unitarian, always accented the last syllable; and as my parents were Episcopalians we followed the Bishop rather than Cousin Charles. At the time of writing the penult accenters are much in a minority.

that the Narrows separating island from mainland are only a hundred paces wide. From the evidence of his map he probably sailed some distance up Blue Hill Bay and then along the coast, naming Isle au Haut, sailed up the Penobscot to the site of Bangor without finding the great city of Norumbega, and returned to the St. Croix, expressing the opinion that Norumbega did not exist. He was right, but not everyone would believe him.

This was Champlain's sole visit to Mount Desert, although he doubtless sighted the island on his later voyage along the New England coast. On his manuscript map of 1607, here reproduced in part, Mount Desert is shown fairly accurately, and named, together with the Cranberry Islands and Bakers and the two Ducks, which are not named. On the west side of Mount Desert he shows indentations that are evidently meant for Seal Cove, Goose Cove and Duck Cove. Bartletts and Hardwood Islands are there too, and the islands of Casco Passage; but Deer Island and the Fox Islands are shown so inaccurately as to suggest that Champlain sailed outside them, past Isle au Haut and Matinicus.

3. The Colony of Saint-Sauveur

SEVERAL years elapsed. Champlain founded Quebec, and his later history is concerned with the lake named after him, and with Canada. De Monts lost his patent, but it was picked up by Antoinette de Pons, Marquise de Guercheville. This lady is distinguished not only for founding the short-lived colony on Mount Desert, but for having been one of the few women to resist the amorous advances of the gallant Henri IV, King Henry of Navarre. After vainly seeking the love of the Marquise when, as an attractive young widow, she served as lady of honor to his Queen, the King arranged to go hunting near her Château de la Roche Guyon. He pretended that he was lost and presented himself, asking hospitality for the night. Madame, warned what to expect, greeted him at the gate beautifully made-up and dressed in her finest court dress and jewels. The King, overcome, cried out, "*Que vois-je, madame; est-ce bien vous, et suis-je ce roi méprisé?*" ("Is this really you, and am I that monarch scorned?") Madame invited him to come in and rest, led him by her hand to the door of her chamber, made a deep curtsy, and retired. Henry, mad with desire, stamped up and down the room, then summoned an equerry, who informed him that Madame la Marquise had caused a sumptuous dinner to be prepared for her would-be royal lover, but had ordered her coach and was about to depart to a friend's château. The King, in great distress, rushed down to the door and called to her, "*Quoi! Madame, je vous chasserai de votre maison?*" ("What! I am driving you from your house?") To which she replied, in a firm tone, "*Sire, un roi doit être le maître partout où il est; et pour moi, je suis bien aise d'avoir quelque pouvoir dans les lieux où je me trouve.*" ("Sir, where a king is, he should be the sole master; but I prefer to keep some little authority wherever I am.")

So the King had to dine, and sleep, without his noble hostess.

It was this lady of laudable if somewhat inconvenient virtue who in 1613 acquired the patent of De Monts, enlarged by Louis XIII to cover the whole of North America to the Gulf of Mexico. At her own expense she dispatched a Jesuit mission to the Indians of Maine. A Jesuit father, Pierre Biard, professor of theology at the University of Lyons, was placed in charge of the mission, which included lay brother Gilbert du Thet, who expressed a desire to die in the New World, and did. The ship was called the *Jonas* — name of ill omen; she was captained by one Flory and the leader of the expedition was the Sieur de la Saussaye.

Their intended destination was the site of Bangor, where they still hoped to find the mythical towers of Norumbega; but fate brought them to Mount Desert. After crossing the Bay of Fundy from Nova Scotia they ran into fog, and then a gale of wind from the southward before which they ran into Frenchmans Bay and anchored. It was now mid-June of 1613. As the wind turned off shore, the sun rose resplendent on a laughing sea, revealing the Porcupine Islands and the wild summits of l'Isle des Monts Déserts. The *Jonas* stood into a sheltered cove — probably either Cromwell or Compass Harbor. There the company landed, a mass was celebrated, and the name Saint-Sauveur given to the place. Presently appeared a few summering Indians, who informed

Father Biard — who had been in Nova Scotia before and could speak Algonkian — that Chief Asticou was sick unto death, and wished to be baptized in time to save his soul.

Asticou, Sagamore of Kenduskeag, the most important chief of the Penobscot branch of the Abnaki, was "a grave man and a goodly presence" according to Lescarbot, the early historian of New France. Father Biard, who knew about him, and was anxious to miss no chance to save a soul, collected all necessary furniture for a baptismal mass, piled into an Indian's canoe, and was paddled past Schooner Head, Great Head, Otter Cliff and across the entrances of Seal Harbor and Northeast Harbor to the entrance of Somes Sound. There, on the present Manchester Point, he found Asticou, who had nothing worse than a bad cold. Having heard well of the French, he wanted them to settle near his summer encampment, and used this ruse to show them the place.

Asticou's savvy salesmanship succeeded. The *Jonas* followed Father Biard under sail. At the sight of Fernalds Point, already covered with a luxuriant growth of grass, jutting into a landlocked bay, with a spring of sweet water bubbling from the beach on either side, and among friendly Indians who wished to be converted, Saussaye and all hands decided "this is it." They gave up the search for fabled Norumbega. The company, about forty in number, disembarked; tents were pitched, trees felled for timber and firewood, ground broken for corn, the men set to work catching and making fish. A score of Indians were baptized. The *Jonas* was securely moored off Fernalds Cove. The name Saint-Sauveur was transferred to this place, a cross was raised with the arms of the Marquise de Guercheville, and mass was said daily.

All went well for three or four weeks; everyone at Saint-

Sauveur, whether Frenchman or Indian, was happy as a clam at high tide. But, alas for the colony, a tough Englishman named Samuel Argall, of the Virginia Colony planted at Jamestown six years earlier, was patrolling the coast in ship *Treasurer* of 14 guns. He had orders to mop up any French settlements between the Hudson and the St. Lawrence, since King James I claimed all that territory for England. Argall would undoubtedly have missed sheltered Saint-Sauveur but for an unfortunate circumstance. Somewhere off Blue Hill Bay the *Treasurer* was boarded by friendly Indians who, innocently assuming that all white men were friends, conveyed to Captain Argall, by a pantomime of genuflections, curtsies and flourishes which could only have been learned from Frenchmen, that a colony of King James's enemies was not far away. Argall expressed a keen desire to visit these polite palefaces, and detained an Indian as pilot.

Next day the *Treasurer* came booming through the Western Way with an east wind on her beam. She was cleared for action, flying a big red battle ensign and a flag with the arms of the Virginia Company, and red canvas waistcloths stretched from fo'c'sle to poop. She whipped around the eastern point of Greenings Island, and bore down before the wind on *Jonas* at anchor. The French ship had nobody on board but the master and a couple of sailors, her unbent sails spread over the deck as awnings.

The French were taken completely by surprise. This was their Pearl Harbor, and there was nobody to blame but themselves. Most of the men, including Saussaye, were ashore; the pilot and some of the sailors, warned by Indians that a ship of warlike aspect was approaching, had launched a boat, but after the pilot got a good look at the *Treasurer* he prudently hid behind Greenings Island. Some half-dozen brave men, including Saussaye's lieutenant La Motte and lay brother Du Thet, hastened on board the *Jonas*, but had no time to bend the sails or weigh anchor before the Englishmen, making a furious din with drums and trumpets, bore down on them and fired a broadside. Captain Flory ordered his men to return fire; but the only one who obeyed was Brother Du Thet. He carried a lighted match to the touch-hole of a cannon, fired the piece without aiming it, and the shot passed harmlessly over the enemy ship. The English replied to this demonstration with a volley of musketry which mortally wounded Du Thet — so he had his wish. Captain Argall ordered "Boarders Away," and in a jiffy his merry men were swarming over the French bulwarks. Lieutenant La Motte tried to fight them off with his broadsword, but he was quickly disarmed and captured. Saussaye and the men ashore, who had neglected to organize any defense, escaped to Flying Mountain and Valley Cove; but after a night in the woods they came out and surrendered.

That was the end of the French colony of Saint-Sauveur. The English plundered their prisoners of everything movable; but at least did not kill them, as the Spaniards had done to the French colony in Florida not long before. Argall gave Saussaye the longboat and told him to shove off; he took fourteen men with him, crossed the Bay of Fundy, met a French ship, and got safely home. The rest, Captain Argall took to Jamestown, where Sir Thomas Dale, Governor of Virginia, threatened to have them hanged as pirates; but Argall successfully interceded and was allowed to carry them to England. Father Biard eventually returned to his academic post at the University of Lyons, where he doubtless entertained his pupils with tales of the beauties of Mount Desert, the kindness of Asticou's Indians, and the cruelty of the English heretics.

4. Mount Desert as a Landmark

THUS began off Fernalds Point a century and a half of rivalry and intermittent warfare between English and French for the possession of North America. King James I of England granted this region to an admiral of the Royal Navy, Sir Robert Mansell, and officially changed the name of Mount Desert to Mount Mansell; but Sir Robert did nothing about it, and the French name stuck.

The greatest importance of Mount Desert for a century and a half was its prominence as a landmark for seamen. Any ship bound from Old England to New England tried to pick up soundings off Nova Scotia, to give both Sable Island and Cape Sable a wide berth, and to cross the Gulf of Maine. If the wind was east or southwest, the ship stood for Mount Agamenticus, behind Old York; but if the wind blew from the west or northwest, the ship made her best course on the port tack across the Bay of Fundy's mouth, which brought her within sight of Mount Desert, whose Green or Cadillac Mountain can be seen sixty miles away in clear weather.

That is what happened to the *Lady Arbella*, flagship of the Winthrop fleet that settled Massachusetts Bay in 1630. Governor Winthrop's journal enables us to plot her course on June 1630; and, on one page of his log, the Puritan governor made the first known sketches of Mount Desert. He sighted the island forty miles northwesterly on 8 June and

altered course to west southwest. "We had now fair sun-
shiny weather," recorded the Governor, "and so pleasant
a sweet air as did much refresh us, and there came a smell
off the shore like the smell of a garden." It was one of those
perfect June days that you often experience in these waters:
a light offshore breeze, fleecy clouds rolling up over the
land; sky, island and ocean in three deepening shades of blue,
and the air filled with the spicy fragrance of early summer
in Maine.

The *Arbella* did not call here; she had been at sea almost
two months, and all hands were anxious to reach Salem and
go ashore. But profiles of the Mount Desert hills are in all
editions of *The English Pilot* from 1706 on; and the 1729
edition shows the Duck Islands, Schooner Head, and Outer
Long Island as well.

5 . Cadillac

BEFORE the end of the seventeenth century another Frenchman turned up at Mount Desert — a brawling, adventurous Gascon whose real name was Antoine Laumet. The son of a village lawyer, he changed his common name to the aristocratic one of La Mothe, and for good measure gave himself the title "Sieur de Cadillac," after a small town near his birthplace. It is from him that our highest mountain has been renamed; and his phony coat of arms, surmounted by a count's coronet that even he did not claim, now decorates the Cadillac car, possession of one or more of which marks the successful business executive or labor union leader.

This self-made gentleman in 1688 obtained a grant from the Governor of Canada to the lordship of Douaquet, described as extending six miles inland, six miles east, and six miles west of the present Sullivan River, together with l'Isle des Monts Déserts. Cadillac and his bride spent a summer or part of a summer in their domain and then departed for reasons unknown, probably for fear that they would meet the fate of the Jesuit colony at the hands of the English. But La Mothe de Cadillac always styled himself "Seigneur de Douaquet et des Monts Déserts." From here he went to Montreal, entered the fur trade, founded Detroit — hence the Cadillac car — and ended his days as Governor of French

Louisiana, an early incumbent of the office lately distinguished by Huey and Earl Long.

Cadillac left in the French royal archives a mémoire describing "The Harbor of Monts Déserts," by which he meant the space between this island and the Cranberries, wherein, he said correctly, "vessels lie as in a box." He mentioned four entrances, the northeastern with nine fathom of water, and the eastern, with fourteen fathom — these are easily identified as the two parts of the Eastern Way, on each side of East Bunkers Ledge. The southeast entrance, he says, has three and a half fathom, but in the channel there's a rock. That must be the Gut between the two Cranberries, but the depth is much less than what he described. The western entrance — the Western Way — says Cadillac, has three and a half fathom, "but to enter safely you must steer west or southwest." The depth is correct for half tide but the direction is wrong; if you steer west inside the Western Way you run on the rocks, as happened to me once in a fog when I mistook the bell buoy in the channel for the gong buoy outside.

Incidentally, it is unfortunate that this name, "The Harbor of Mount Desert" or "The Great Harbor of Mount Desert," has gone out. It appears in an Act of Congress of 7 July 1838 authorizing the building of Bear Island lighthouse "at the entrance of Mount Desert Harbor," but I have never found it on any map or chart. The name ought to be revived.

In the meantime King James II of England had scrambled all English colonies east of Pennsylvania into the Dominion of New England, and appointed Sir Edmund Andros his governor. In the summer of 1688, Sir Edmund cruised Down East in His Majesty's frigate *Rose* to inspect the frontier, and made a census of all Europeans living east of the Penobscot. On Eggemoggin Reach he found a French couple and a single man. On an island he calls "Pettit Pleasure by Mount Desert" were two English couples named Hind and Lowrey and their children; and at "Winskeage Bay, on the eastern side of Mount Desert," the Cadillacs. "Pettit Pleasure" means Gotts Island, which up to a century and a half ago was called Little Placentia. Winskeage Bay may mean almost anything between Otter Creek and Schoodic Peninsula; but the fact that Schooner Head is called "Windscot Point" on the English *Coast Pilot* of 1729 suggests that the Cadillacs camped on the eastern coast of the Island. In any case, the Cadillacs soon left, and what became of the Lowreys and Hinds we know not.

For seventy-five years there was no permanent settlement on Mount Desert Island. Not that it was deserted. Frenchmans Bay was so called because it became a staging point for French warships preparing to fight the English. At the same time English warships used what Cadillac called the Harbor of Mount Desert, inside the Cranberries. Sailors found this island just the place to replenish with fish, firewood, and fresh water. A stream which drains the valley between Robinson (Acadia) and Dog (St. Sauveur) Mountains is called Man o' War Brook to this day, because English warships used to fill their water casks where the stream tumbles over granite ledges into Somes Sound.

So we may imagine Eagle Cliff in the eighteenth century echoing the martial airs of England as the King's colors were raised at the opening of forenoon watch and lowered at sunset; whilst, on the other side of the Island, Indians peering through the woods around Bar Harbor could see the white ensign of France floating from the flagstaffs of French frigates, admire the noble strains of the royal anthem *Vexilla*

Regis coming over the water, and hear ships' bells striking the half-hours day and night.

In 1740 there occurred a fatal wreck on Long Ledge at the entrance to the Western Way. The great ship *Grand Design*, bearing scores of men and women from Ulster to settle in Pennsylvania, was carried far off her course by a southerly gale, and crashed on the ledge. Many there were drowned; others got away in the ship's boats and put in at a little cove east of Bass Harbor Head, now called Ship Harbor. A company of young men struck out to the mainland seeking succor, and were never heard from again. After the shipwrecked people had been living on clams and blueberries for months, some friendly Indians passed by, gave them corn and carried the news of their plight to the little English settlement at the site of Warren, on the St. Georges River above Thomaston, which sent a vessel for their relief. Two Irish widows whose husbands had died of starvation at Ship Harbor married two young men of Warren, Archibald Gamble and John McCarter, and from them hundreds of Maine Gambles and Carters are descended.

6. The New England Settlement Begins

B Y 1760 the French and Indian wars were over, and with them the danger of Indian raids on the New England frontiers. For, now that their French protectors had withdrawn from North America, the genial Abnaki summer resorters of Mount Desert folded their tents like the Arabs and silently stole away — to Quoddy, to Old Town, and to the deep woods; whence some of their descendants, like those described by Adelma Joy, occasionally returned to hunt, fish and make and sell baskets.

Now, for the first time, the New England people began systematic settlement of their easternmost border. There appeared opportunely on the scene Francis Bernard, Royal Governor of the Province of the Massachusetts Bay, one of those Englishmen who came out to the colonies to do good — and did well, up to a point. The land speculators of Boston, who had not yet thought of calling themselves "realtors," wished to lay out townships along Eggemoggin Reach, the Union River and Mount Desert Narrows; but Massachusetts had been forbidden by the King to grant land in eastern Maine, which he was half-minded to annex to Nova Scotia. Governor Bernard had a wife and ten children to provide for, and he wanted a piece of those eastern lands; so the colonial legislators contrived with him a political clambake.

They granted the Island of Mount Desert to the Governor, and the other townships to deserving patriots like James Otis, all in the same bill; the joker being that if Governor Bernard obtained special permission from George III to acquire Mount Desert, the royal grace would cover their speculations as well.

The deal worked and Governor Bernard became sole proprietor of the Island of Mount Desert in 1764. But he did not wait for the royal O.K. to do something about securing his claim. In 1761 he induced Abraham Somes and James Richardson of Gloucester to start a settlement, offering them plenty of land free. The Governor had heard that Somes and Ebenezer Sutton had visited the Island in 1755, when Somes bought Greenings Island from an Indian summering there for a gallon of rum, and Sutton made an even better bargain, acquiring a birch-bark deed to the island that bears his name for only two quarts. Somes and Richardson settled in the summer of 1761 at what is now Somesville, originally called by the picturesque name "Betwixt the Hills." Thus, the year 1961 marks the bicentenary of permanent settlement on Mount Desert Island, although Somes did not bring up his wife and children until the following spring.

In September 1762, Governor Bernard cruised Down East in the official sloop *Massachusetts*, with guns mounted and a uniformed crew, to view his expected domain. Taking a pilot at Naskeag Harbor, he entered the "Great Harbour" by the Western Way (taking two hours to beat in against a head wind) and anchored in "South West Harbour" on 2 October. He found that in addition to the Someses and Richardsons at the head of the Sound (Mrs. Somes he described as a "notable woman" and her four daughters as "pretty girls, neat and orderly"), there were several uninvited settlers — doubtless the Spurlings, Stanleys, Bunkers and Hadlocks — on Great and Little Cranberry. Stephen Richardson was living at Bass Harbor, and there were two or three families at Southwest Harbor. These last, however, were not permanent settlers; William Gilley, the first who really stayed, arrived some thirty years later. The Governor caused the land around Southwest Harbor to be surveyed and laid out in house and pasture lots. He gave each family already there a deed to his lot, and built two or more houses for them. The General Court had the entire coast from Owls Head to Petit Manan surveyed in 1765, producing a map which gives a remarkably accurate outline of Mount Desert and neighboring islands, in some respects better than Holland's of the next decade.

But the American Revolution caught up with the Governor and ruined his plans. The patriots made it so uncomfortable for him that he returned to England, where the King rewarded him by the title of Baronet. During the course of the war all his American property was confiscated, and Mount Desert Island was thrown into hotchpot.

In 1772, Samuel Holland, official British surveyor for North America, made a chart of Mount Desert Island which is copied in the British Album known as *The Atlantic Neptune*. Almost every cove and brook is entered, and the few houses already built are spotted in: six at Bar Harbor and Hulls Cove, four at Somesville, two at Southwest Harbor, four on the Cranberries and one on Bartletts Island. Northeast Harbor, curiously enough, is left out. Fog must have concealed the harbor entrance on the day that Holland sailed by.

Captain William Owen RN, founder of the settlement on Campobello Island, New Brunswick, wrote an amusing account of a cruise to Mount Desert in 1770. His schooner *Campo-Bello* was piloted by Aaron Bunker of Cranberry Island. She dropped anchor in Cranberry Harbor on 27 October. Bunker's parents, with some of their younger children and grandchildren, were settled on Great Duck Island; his brother John lived on Little Cranberry, and another brother and married sister on Great Cranberry; "the lads" (says Captain Owen) "all healthy, robust and industrious; the lasses fair, handsome and good-natured." One of them, the pilot's sister Mary, was a little too good-natured for Aaron's taste. He found her in bed, bundling with one of Owen's shipmates, who is described as a wealthy settler of Deer Island named Eaton. The upshot was a hasty marriage between Eaton and Miss Bunker, performed by Captain Owen in his capacity as shipmaster, there being no minister or justice of the peace available within thirty miles. "A good substantial, and plentiful entertainment was provided," writes the impromptu parson, "and a real and genuine Yankee frolic ensued."

Captain Owen next made Bass Harbor, where he found "two poor, honest, industrious families settled," the Stephen Richardsons and Job Dennings. The latters' daughter he described as "a fine girl" who "in a very few years will be able to spin, card and do as her mama did before her." He sailed as far as Portland, and on his return passage called once more at Little Cranberry and married a member of his crew "to one Mary Wright, a buxome widow," and "the evening was spent in Yankey jiggs and country-dances, much innocent mirth and social glee."

At the end of the War of Independence two claimants for Mount Desert Island came forward. One was the Governor's son, Sir John Bernard, who had joined the winning side of the Revolution. He petitioned the General Court of Massachusetts (to which Maine belonged until 1820) to have the whole of his father's island restored to him. The other was Madame Barthelmy de Grégoire, granddaughter of the self-styled Sieur de Cadillac. This lady, a simple-minded but grasping Frenchwoman about forty years old, came to Boston in 1786 with three children and her husband, bearing letters of introduction from Lafayette and other important people, and demanding her grandfather's lordship of Douaquet. Since this was our honeymoon period with France, the Bay State solons were agreeable. With one stroke of the pen, they naturalized the De Grégoires; with another they gave the lady the eastern half of Mount Desert Island and a section of adjoining mainland; and with a third they confirmed the western half of the Island to Sir John Bernard as a reward for sticking to our side when his father stood by the King.

So this island now belonged in part to an English baronet, son of a royal governor of Massachusetts Bay; and in part to the granddaughter of Cadillac.

The division of the island was made along Somes Sound and a line northwest from Doctor Kittredge's brook to Indian Point on Blue Hill Bay. Bernard took the western half and Madame de Grégoire the eastern, and from one or the other all titles on the Island are derived. Sir John promptly mortgaged his share to Thomas Russell of Boston, and returned to England, where he made his peace with the King and obtained a job in the colonial service in the West Indies. The first survey of this western half, made in 1806 by a Massachusetts man with the unusual name of Salem Town, is preserved in the Mount Desert Museum at Somesville. Almost every one of the families named therein as owning a hundred-acre lot has descendants of the same name on the

Island today. John Manchester, for instance, settled in 1775 at Northeast Harbor, which is still full of Manchesters.

The De Grégoires settled at Hulls Cove, where the Hamor, Young and Hull families had established themselves before the War of Independence. Madame made a poor and precarious living granting deeds to squatters, at five dollars per one hundred acres, or selling at a slightly higher rate. In 1792 she sold most of her vast asset in scenery to Henry Jackson of Boston for £1247 16s, and Jackson in turn sold out to William Bingham of Philadelphia.

About that time a very forthright and energetic French gentlewoman appeared on the scene. This was Madame Bacler de Leval, *émigrée* from the French Revolution, with a retinue of friends and servants. From Madame de Grégoire she bought land along the Jordan and Skilling Rivers, and planned to establish, on the shores of Mount Desert Narrows and Taunton Bay, an American center of French enterprise and culture. By a curious but fitting coincidence, M. Pierre Monteux has established a summer school of music on land once owned by her. In the town of Lamoine, named after one of Madame's followers, one can still see the site of her home lot, "Fontaine Leval," marked by a row of Lombardy poplars, grown from shoots of trees that she planted. This colony did not last long; but the colonists left some distinguished descendants — the La Farge and De Laittre families, and the Des Isles, who remained here and anglicized their name as Desizzle.

When Madame de Grégoire died in 1811 the rest of her land, like Henry Jackson's and some of Sir John Bernard's on the western side, passed to Senator William Bingham of Philadelphia, one of the wealthiest Americans of the early Republic. From him it passed to the Bingham Trust, representing several Philadelphia families and the house of Baring in London. The first person to profit by these speculations was Colonel John Black, agent of the Binghams and Barings — of which his mansion at Ellsworth is good evidence. Gradually the Bingham Trust sold off their land on Mount Desert, but as recently as 1950 they still held about fifty acres on the eastern half of the island.

There were other ephemeral speculations in Mount Desert lands. One of these brought to Island shores, as prospector, none other than Charles Maurice de Talleyrand-Périgord, sometime bishop of Autun, and later Prince de Bénévent and Emperor Napoleon's right-hand man. He came to seek land for a group of French refugees from the Reign of Terror, but decided not to buy. His presence, however, gave rise to a strange myth that he was born on the Island. It seems to have arisen because someone who saw him strolling about said, "That fellow looks like the little French bastard who was running around Southwest Harbor thirty years ago." Actually, Talleyrand's birth and early years in France are as well documented as John Adams's in Massachusetts; and except for the few days spent ashore, he had nothing to do with Mount Desert. His impressions of the inhabitants were unfavorable. He states that coin was so scarce that pins were used for small change, "even for prostitution." Can this be the origin of the phrase "I don't care two pins for her"?

7. The People of Mount Desert

A MUCH brighter picture of the first permanent settlers on the Island is given by Bancel de Confoulens, who visited it in the summer of 1792. Prospecting for another group of Frenchmen who wished to emigrate, he traveled through the Narrows and along the shore to Bar Harbor. "I saw very well kept houses," he wrote, "and settlers honest, affable and generous," living at about the same standard as the people in Philadelphia and Boston, all having fine healthy children. "These inhabitants cultivate enough land to provide themselves with potatoes, corn, barley and vegetables, but they spend most of their time cutting wood into shooks and barrel staves which they sell at good profit to merchants. Each family has a small boat from which they catch cod, and cure it, and exchange it with the merchants for flour, sugar, soap, molasses, oil and other articles that they want. All have cows and farmyards, poultry of every kind and fine pigs. They make cheese which they sell at wholesale. On the day of my arrival there were five ships in Frenchmans Bay, one of which sailed for London, one for Santo Domingo, and three for Boston, loaded with plank, timber, shooks, bark, and even cordwood, which the people cut on the edge of the bays or in the forest." The only thing the people lacked, he observed, was a supply of salt; they offered to exchange two pounds of fresh beef, veal, pork, lamb or turkey, for one pound of salt meat out of the ship's "harness cask."

An equally favorable account of the Mount Desert settlers was written four years later, in 1796, by young Alexander Baring, who almost half a century later, as Lord Ashburton, negotiated the Maine-Canada boundary treaty with Daniel Webster. Baring, representing the English banking house of that name which lent Senator Bingham money for his investments and speculations, married Ann Louise, daughter of the Senator; later her sister Maria married Alexander's younger brother Henry Baring.

In June 1796 Alexander Baring accompanied the Binghams and their two daughters, the Vicomte de Noailles (a French *émigré*) and John Richards (founder of the distinguished family of Gardiner) in a cruise Down East. The Senator chartered a packet sloop at Portland. They called on General Knox at his new mansion "Montpelier" at Thomaston, and viewed the country thereabouts; then left the ladies at "Montpelier" and sailed eastward. They passed through "Edgemogin Reach," [1] crossed Bass Harbor bar, and sailed past Bakers Island to Gouldsborough, where they met General David Cobb; thence to Passamaquoddy Bay and up the St. Croix to Calais, where they were plagued by "the immensity of Musketoes." Returning westward they sailed up Frenchmans Bay and through the Narrows into Blue Hill Bay, up the Union River to Ellsworth, then called at Bartletts Island and obtained a supply of mutton, vegetables and dairy products from the pioneer Christopher Bartlett, whom they reported to be "at open war" with his neighbors on Mount Desert. This "war" was over his cutting hay on the salt meadows at Prettymarsh. That was a frequent source of

[1] This, incidentally, is how Eggemoggin Reach is spelled in most of the early accounts and maps, and how it should be pronounced.

trouble in the early days, because settlers who owned no salt meadow in their hundred-acre lots felt that they had a right to procure their winter forage wherever they could find it, and the owners objected.

Alexander Baring, who had earlier visited the Genesee Valley of New York and the Pennsylvania frontier, reported that the settlers of Eastern Maine were vastly superior in character to the western pioneers. He observed that their first wants after satisfying bare necessities were a church and a school; whilst in the Genesee "the bulk of settlers are ignorant and destitute of all of morality."

He also noted that the people of Eastern Maine were stanch supporters of Washington's administration. It is indeed remarkable that during the life of the Federalist party a majority of the people of Hancock and Washington Counties almost invariably supported it, and in later years went Whig and Republican, having little use for Jeffersonian or Jacksonian Democracy; for this fact runs completely counter to the theory that the American frontier was democratic and radical.

Although the people of Southwest Harbor valiantly drove off a landing party from H.M.S. *Tenedos* in 1813, and George Harman, member of the General Court from the town of Mount Desert, voted against calling the Hartford Convention, there were many English sympathizers on the Island and in Eastern Maine. This was natural, in view of the unfriendliness of the Jefferson and Madison administrations to maritime interests. Robert Snowman, an uncle of Captain Lorenzo Stewart of Seal Cove, who went to Castine during the war to work in a shipyard, died from a beating administered by local "Tories" because he refused to drink a toast to King George. But Nat Dyer, given a similar invitation, offered this sentiment:

Here's a health to King George, God damn him;
May the crows pick his eyes, and hang him,
And drive him all round the ramparts of hell,
              God damn him!

And Nat, being a stout fellow, was not molested.

Dr. Kittredge of Somesville, the pioneer physician on the Island, whose services used to be summoned by signal fires on the hills, was also a "Tory" of 1812. He told Captain Stewart's father that this country would be no good until its laws were like those of England. "Why," he said, "when my dotters goes t' meetin' there's nothin' t' distinguish 'em from the common people!" In later years Dr. Kittredge built himself a tomb. His rival physician, Dr. Damon, managed to shut him up in it during the better part of a day, and he caught a cold which developed into a consumption from which he died.

Thus, the settlement of Mount Desert Island was well under way before 1800, and had taken on the character that still persists on the western side of the Island, despite an overlay of tourist and summer-colony interests. By 1860 or 1880 almost every square rod of land that could be improved for cornfield, hayfield or pasture, and every possible site for a saw or grist mill, had been taken up. The settlers came largely from Cape Ann, Cape Cod, and southern Maine; and they came by sea, mostly in Chebacco boats, the little double-ended type of pinkie schooner with no bowsprit that originated in the Chebacco parish of Ipswich, later Essex. They were representative pioneers of that mixed breed, the Yankee. Most of them, like the Manchesters, Kimballs, Someses and Higginses, were of English stock; others, like the Gilpatricks, Fenellys and Murphys, were Irish; the Stanleys and Savages were Scotch; the Obers and Lurveys had a remote German background, and there were some odd combinations, like the Lynams of Bar Harbor, descendants of a Prussian girl and a French army officer. James Richardson, fellow pioneer at Somesville with Abraham Somes, was the offspring of an early *Lady Chatterley's Lover* affair. His father, head gardener to a Scots laird, secretly married his employer's daughter, Lady Jane Montgomery; they eloped to America, and James was their son. There is even said to be considerable Russian blood on the "back side" [2] of the Island, deriving from a six months' visit to Southwest Harbor by auxiliary cruiser *Cimbria* of the Imperial Russian Navy. This was in 1878, when war was threatened between Russia and England. She had seven hundred sailors on board, and one hundred at a time were given shore liberty; it may be presumed that they made a few conquests. Incidentally, the *Cimbria* was the last warship to replenish her water supply at Man o' War Brook.

The economy of the Island settlers was based on forest and sea. By 1870, almost the entire first growth of timber was cut off, if not burned down, to make lumber, ship timber and cordwood. Schooners and brigs were built in every cove and harbor. These vessels were built by local men, on shares sometimes as small as one sixty-fourth. Some were employed fishing on the banks; others carried cordwood and lumber to Eastern cities between Portland and Baltimore; a

---

[2] The "back side of Mount Desert" originally was applied to the rocky outer coast, from Bar Harbor to Somes Sound; but more recently it has been used for the opposite Blue Hill Bay shore, which was not favored by summer colonists. There is a wonderful old ballad about deadly doings on this "back side" which I heard sung, years ago, by Uncle Juddy Carver at Lakeman's Harbor, Roque Island; if anyone knows the words he will confer a favor on me by letting me have them.

few traded to the West Indies and South America — source of the conch shells you see in many old houses today. Some of the earliest yachts kept at Northeast Harbor, such as schooners *Fanny Earl* and *Merry Chanter*, were built on Suttons Island.

The town of Tremont, which then included Southwest Harbor, had a population of 1800 in 1871. Among them were six ship contractors, five boatbuilders, three master and thirteen plain ship carpenters, four ship joiners, eight calkers and gravers, one sailmaker and one rigger. These were the professionals; but it is safe to say that almost every man could lend a hand at hewing out ship timber.

On the west side of Bartletts Island is a place called Brig Landing Cove, which records the loss of the hermaphrodite brig *Emmeline*, Captain David Bartlett. Returning in ballast from the West Indies, she was becalmed in Blue Hill Bay, but the captain and crew were so anxious to see their wives on the other side of the island that they warped the brig into this little cove, anchored her and walked home. Let us hope that they had a warm welcome; for their gallantry cost them dear. That night, a northwest gale blew up and *Emmeline* tripped her anchor and drifted hard and fast aground. The exotic flint-rock ballast that she brought from the West Indies was thrown overboard in an endeavor to float her. If you don't believe me, you can see it there yet, at a low "dreen o' tide."

Some of these schooners were very fast. Simeon Milliken's cordwood packet, after discharging her cargo at South Boston one summer day in the 1870's, set sail for her home port, Seal Cove, just at sunrise. There was a brisk northwest wind, the schooner had no cargo, and Captain Milliken carried all the sail she had — mainsail, foresail and jib. One Richardson, the only other member of the crew, was stationed at the foresheet; but he was deaf; so, when Milliken halloed to let out the sheet, he pretended not to hear and shouted aft: "Don't slack off yet, Cap'n, she'll stand it!" Stand it she did, and before dark that night the schooner anchored off Dodges Point. Figure it out for yourself; I make it that, even if this famous passage was made on the longest day of the year, she averaged 10½ knots.

On shore, men set up smokehouses for herring which the fishermen caught off the Magdalen Islands. Apparently herring did not favor our harbors in those days, but the long-since departed porgy or menhaden did, and many try-houses were built for extracting the oil, which brought a good price. The men cleared their farms of trees and boulders, first pasturing the land with sheep and neat cattle, then turning the better parts into tillage. They grew wheat, rye and corn, and vast quantities of Irish potatoes, whose vines were still free from the Colorado beetle. The women carded, spun and wove their own wool for clothing, kept poultry, made cheese and butter, tended a vegetable garden. Every family "made" a few "cords" of dried pollock and cod, and pickled a few barrels of mackerel, for winter use; and the men supplemented this homely fare by wild fowl and venison.

These Mount Desert people were the handiest in the world at turning a liability into an asset. The round, smooth stones on sea walls, such as those at Hunters Beach and Bracys Cove, were just what cities wanted for paving streets; you can still see these "popplestones," as they were called on the Island (cobblestones elsewhere), in Louisburg Square, Boston. Ice cut on the Island ponds brought a good price until artificial ice became easy to make. Ice House Hill on Harbourside Road, Northeast Harbor, recalls the wooden ice railway from Lower Hadlock Pond which passed under the road by a tunnel to a wharf on Northeast Harbor. I can remember a schooner loading there for New York, and the men pushing great blocks of ice along the wooden trestle and giving them a shove through the tunnel. At the heyday of the national demand for granite, Hall's Quarry on Somes Sound was very productive, providing stone for public buildings as far west as Omaha; and smaller quarries were established on the opposite side of the Sound, on Eagle Lake, on Black Island and elsewhere. The carriage of this stone to major seaports or railheads provided schooners with profitable freights; the last of them, the old *Bloomer*, which plied these waters for a good half-century carrying "stun," had her masts widely spaced to afford maximum hatches, and her fore gaff doubled as derrick.

Your true Mount Deserter disproved the old adage, "Jack of all trades, master of none." He could be fisherman, sailor, farmer, lumberman, shipwright and quarryman rolled into one, and master of all. Augustus C. Savage and his father cut two hundred cords of wood in the winter of 1850–1851, hauled them to their wharf in Northeast Harbor, and shipped them to Boston in their own schooner. She was caught in the severe storm that destroyed the first lighthouse on Minot's Ledge, but made Portsmouth safely and delivered her cargo. My old friend Wilbur Herrick, known principally as a good horseman and keeper of a livery stable, was also an expert blacksmith, turning out articles in wrought iron which we are proud to own today. I have watched Wilbur Herrick select a straight hickory tree in the woods, square off a balk about three feet long, split it longitudinally into four sticks of equal size, and fashion each into a beau-

CHAMPLAIN'S 1607 CHART OF MAINE COAST
Section from the Kennebec River to Machias Bay

Isles perdues — Long or Fox Is.
Norumbegue — the fabled city
pentegoet — Penobscot Bay
Isle haute — Isle au Haut
orsènes Isles — Matinicus

I. monts desers — Mount Desert
menanan — Petit Manan
C. de cornolles — Great Wass I.
Isles ranges — The Roque I. group

VIEW FROM KIMBALL HOUSE, NORTHEAST HARBOR, 1884
St. Mary's Chapel, Bishop Doane's cottage, and Cornings' "Stone Ac

SCENE IN BAR HARBOR, 1886
Steamer *Mount Desert* at left; steamer *Sappho* leering over roof of w

Photo taken in 1890

FERNALDS POINT, SITE OF THE SAINT-SAUVEUR MISSION, 1613

MOUNT DESERT, FROM LITTLE CRANBERRY ISLAND

Photo by W. H. Ballard, Southwest Harbor

THE MACKEREL FLEET IN SOUTHWEST HARBOR

YOUNG LADIES ON A "TEAKETTLE" PARTY, 1902

Studio photo of c. 1900   *Snapshot by author, c. 1925, on the porch of his cottage*

FOUNDERS OF THE NORTHEAST HARBOR SUMMER COLONY

Left: William Croswell Doane, Bishop of Albany
Right: Charles William Eliot, President of Harvard University

Photo by W. H. Ballard, Southwest

BAR HARBOR AND FRENCHMANS BAY, FROM CADILLAC MOUNTAIN

OTTER CLIFFS

The reef at extreme left is the one where Cadillac struck

Photo by W. H. Ballard, Southwest

THE FOUR HIGGINSES, PROPRIETORS OF BAR HARBOR HOTELS

ephen, Albert, Charles and Sam, each a hotel proprietor in 1873

JORDAN'S POND AND THE BUBBLES, ABOUT 1890

e sign reads "Boats to Let: 25 cts. pr. Hour, 15 cts. pr. Half Hour.
Please Settle at the Office"

Abram Gilpatrick's Friendship Sloop *Alma*
Sailing out of Gilpatrick's Cove, about 1895

An International and a Luders Jockeying for the Start, o
Northeast Harbor

tifully balanced ax-handle. And all done with no other tools but an ax and a drawknife.

Bass Harbor, Southwest Harbor and Cranberry Harbor became prosperous fishing ports; together they owned eighty-five sail, with an aggregate tonnage of 6384 in 1837. The paddle steamboat *Maine*, built by fastening two schooners' hulls together, catamaran fashion, plied between Portland and Eastport as early as 1824, calling at Cranberry Isles; the passage took five days, as she spent the nights in harbor. An endless procession of coasting craft passed by: the bald-headed "johnny wood boats" carrying firewood from the upper St. John River to the Rockland lime kilns; big lumber schooners bound from the St. Croix to Boston and New York; two-masted schooners carrying general cargoes; three- and four-masted schooners carrying coal. The favorite inside route from the Maritime Provinces to Boston passed through the Eastern Way, the Western Way, Casco Passage, Deer Island and Fox Island thoroughfares, and Two Bush Channel. The mackerel fishing fleet from Gloucester, a hundred sail of beautiful tall schooners, each carrying two gaff-topsails, was a marvelous sight as it filled Southwest or Cranberry Harbor.

There were an incredible number of these sailing vessels. The 1854 edition of Blount's *Coast Pilot* states that as many as 400 sail had been in Southwest Harbor at one time, taking refuge from a blow. Captain Joseph Smith USN reported to the Secretary of the Treasury in 1837 that "over 600 sail" had been counted in "Mount Desert Harbor" and its "inlets" at one time. Charles Tracy counted 55 vessels under sail from Sargent Mountain one August day in 1855, and then got tired of counting; he estimated that three or four times that number were then within sight. Yet all this went on with scarcely any help in the way of aids to navigation. The light on Bakers Island was established in 1828, the one on Mount Desert Rock two years later. The Bear Island light goes back to 1839, when Captain Smith recommended it as an excellent guide for both the Eastern and the Western Way. There is on record at Washington a petition signed by some fifty inhabitants of Mount Desert to the Secretary of the Treasury in 1830 to buoy Greenings Island Ledge, a hazard for vessels entering Southwest Harbor or Somes Sound; but they had to wait over forty years to get that. The first daymark established by the government was the pyramidical stone beacon on East Bunkers Ledge, built in 1839–1840 at a cost of under a thousand dollars. The first three buoys in these waters, for which Congress passed a special act in 1838, were set out to mark the ledges at the entrances to Northeast and Bass Harbors. They cost the taxpayer only fifty dollars each.

Thus, all this commercial sailing, and the earliest steaming too, was conducted with little or no help from the government. It is not surprising that one found almost every few miles along the shore the wreck of a vessel that had missed her way in fog or darkness.

Such was the life here before the decline of sailing ships and wooden shipbuilding, and the coming of the "rusticator," transformed the economy of Mount Desert Island. This life found classic expression in Eliot's *John Gilley, Maine Farmer and Fisherman*. I would guess that this farming and seafaring economy reached its height in the 1880's. The Colby-Stuart map of the Island in 1887 shows twelve houses on the road between Seal Cove and Norwoods Cove, where there are none today, and twenty-one houses on the Cape Road, where today there are only three summer cottages. At that time there was perhaps ten times as much cleared land along the coast as there is now; after the original growth had been cut off for timber or cordwood a tract bordering on the shore would be fenced on the land side and used as pasture. These rocky shore pastures had a beauty, to my way of thinking, far surpassing the massed groves of spruce and hardwood that the summer people allowed to grow up, after they bought these properties. The close-cropped grass, the purple rhodora and blueberry blossoms in June, the pink sheep laurel in July, the asters and goldenrod in August, growing around and between the decaying stumps, had a peculiar charm. Songbirds loved these clearings; one of my earliest recollections is hearing a flock of white-throated sparrows singing their "Old Sam Peabody! Peabody! Peabody!" in Captain Sans Whitmore's pasture, which is now a spruce forest. In almost every level spot of the Island, farmers had grubbed out the rocks to make a hayfield, since hay was their fuel for transportation and milk; but now those open fields, where the redtop and timothy grew mixed with all kinds of wild flowers, are a thing of the past. Hay is no longer wanted, and these fields too have reverted to wilderness.

The inhabitants of Mount Desert had character and guts. They were a God-fearing people. Captain Samuel Gilpatrick of Northeast Harbor, where there was no church, used to row across the Sound to Norwoods Cove and walk six miles to Center, to attend meeting on Sunday. They were naturally intelligent if not intellectual; natural navigators with compasses built into their heads; natural teachers, too, for they passed along to their children and to us newcomers some of that art and mystery of the sea which they had learned the hard way, in the days of sail and sweep. It was a privilege to grow up as I did with men such as Abram Gilpatrick and Lewis Stanley to teach me to row and sail; and to know intimately men like Captain Lorenzo Stewart, Robert Dow and Alfred Butler, who knew the ways of ships and birds and fish, and the land and all growing things. Mount Deserters above all were friendly and kindly people, always ready to turn-to and help neighbor or stranger in need; an inheritance from the days when pioneer isolation and loneliness made human kindness more valued than anything else. I hope that we summer visitors from heavily populated regions, where courtesy and friendliness have been almost crowded out, may absorb something of those human qualities which, over and above the magnificent scenery, make Mount Desert to me, after almost seventy summers, still fresh, exciting, and a blessed country.

Although education on the Island, to 1875, was largely confined to the "three R's," it must not be supposed that the people were dull clods — far from it. Many of the men who "sailed foreign" knew the coasts of the West Indies and South America intimately. Captain Asa Smallidge of Northeast Harbor was wont to say that the world's only harbor to equal our Great Harbor was that of Rio de Janeiro. When in 1915 there was talk of the Royal Navy forcing the Dardanelles, Albert Reynolds told me how he had seen, from his brig, the British Mediterranean Squadron come through the Dardanelles under full sail, in 1878. Nathaniel S. Shaler, the geologist, told of an interesting encounter with a farmer who taught himself Greek. That was in 1860, when Shaler with other college students was working for the Coast Survey in a small open sloop. One night they anchored in the little bight at the north end of Ironbound Island in Frenchmans Bay. They saw one house there, up a hill. Shaler was sent to request food and lodging. Seated outside the house was an old man reading aloud from a book something that sounded to Shaler like unintelligible jargon. Shaler stated his wants; the old man replied by handing him the book, saying "Can you read this?" It was the New Testament in Greek, which the old fellow had taught himself to read, assigning his own sounds to the Greek letters. After Shaler had read a few verses — for all college students in those days knew Greek — the farmer said he and his friends could stay as long as they liked, if they would teach him the language; and for three days they took turns at tutoring the old fellow intensively. He caught on to Greek grammar and pronunciation remarkably quickly; and as the boys sailed away they could see the old man sitting on the shore, book in hand, delightedly roaring out the grand opening verses of the Gospel according to St. John.

The people of Mount Desert, as soon as they were numerous enough, organized Congregational and Baptist churches, schools, and friendly societies. They also wrote their own poetry — ballads which were sung in the country stores or around the home fires. Many were collected by Fanny Eckstorm; many more have been forgotten. Here are a few of the verses about Lew Bracey, the bad boy of the Cranberry Islands, which Mrs. Eckstorm took down from Mary Hamor many years ago. They are sung to the tune of an old English ballad "Robin on the Moor," and tell the true story of an episode in the 1860's:

BRACEY ON THE SHORE

It was a young captain, on Cranberry Isles did dwell;
He took the schooner *Arnold*, I suppose you all know well.
She was a tops'l schooner and hailed from Calais, Maine;
They took a load from Boston to cross the ranging main.

CHORUS
Bracey on the shore, Bracey on the shore,
Bold and undaunted stood Lew Bracey on the shore.

He arrived to Cranberry Island and anchored off the P'int,
The wind was to the east'ard, a blowin' feather-white.
The *Arnold* dragged her anchor and drifted on the Bar;
They tried all means to get her off, but couldn't move a spar.

They had a little miss on board, I do not know her name,
They took her out of prison, all down to Calais, Maine.
They say she was part Indian, but that I do not know,
But when the *Arnold* struck adrift, it proved her overthrow.

They say that Captain Boardman has just arrived in town;
He says that Captain Bracey is the biggest rogue he's found.
Up speaks the other gentleman and says we'll have to stop,
For she's loaded with gin bottles from her keel up to her top.

Cynthy took a firkin full and lugged them way round home
To decorate her cupboard all in the no'theast room.
She says "Now dearest Lewis, pray do not drink no more,
For folks are talking very bad all down around the shore."

They say that Mrs. Howard has got a case of gin;
She deals it out for medicine to cheat the eyes of men.
Aunt Barkis says, "I vanny! I think it's very good
To have a little whiskey, when Amos's cuttin' wood."

The way he's got his livin' is smugglin' tea and gin
Across St. Stephen River up to Bar Harbor, Maine.
And now it's Captain Bracey, I'll tell you what to do;
It's leave off drinkin' whiskey, and huggin' the women too!

CHORUS
Bracey on the shore, Bracey on the shore,
Bold and undaunted stood Lew Bracey on the shore.

Given this background, it is not surprising that the Mount Deserters, as soon as educational opportunities opened, profited by them. Beginning with Dr. Merritt L. Fernald, the eminent Harvard botanist, there have been a succession of professors, such as Dr. Ralph R. Ober of the Harvard Medical School and Dean John E. Stewart of the University of

Maine, who were born and brought up on this Island; and now we have a college president too, Dr. Asa Smallidge Knowles of Northeastern University. Even before the generation that produced them, the speech of the Mount Deserters was remarkably correct as well as muscular and virile — instinctively they used shall and will, should and would, correctly. And, in the ordinary pursuits of farm and fishing, *le mot juste*. "How are you going to get that canoe over to Prettymarsh?" a farmer once asked me. "Haul it," I said. "Would you like me to lend you my haywagon?" "No, thanks, I can take it on my back." "Oh, you mean you are going to *carry* it!"

Obsolete words were sometimes used in a vigorous way, such as the verb to "scoff," meaning to scoop or gobble up something. The owner and master of a lobster smack was crossing the Gulf of Maine. The other member of the crew, at the wheel, pointed out a black cloud making up; suggested they reef down. "Oh, the moon'll scoff it up," said the skipper, and turned in. The squall broke, the mainsail was torn to shreds, and the skipper came boiling up on deck. "Where's the mainsail?" he said to the hand. "Oh, the moon scoffed it up!"

8. The Rusticators

NEWPORT in Rhode Island became a summer resort as early as the mid-eighteenth century, but nobody thought of Mount Desert in that connection until artists began coming here in the late 1840's. Hitherto, if anyone, French, English or American, had admired our scenery, he made no record of it. Mount Desert was gloomy, sinister, forbidding, as Whittier put it in his "Mogg Megone":

> The gray and thunder-smitten pile
> Which marks afar the Desert Isle —

— a gross libel on Mount Desert, which has fewer thunderstorms than any other resort in New England — and again:

> There, gloomily against the sky
> The Dark Isles rear their summits high;
> And Desert Rock, abrupt and bare,
> Lifts its gray turrets in the air.

A completely contrary attitude was that of the first artists who visited the island. These men, of the Hudson River School of American painters, were the first to find beauty in American scenery. Their initial efforts were in the valley of the Hudson, but they soon began going far afield in search of subjects; and in 1844 Thomas Cole, a leader of the school, came to the Island to sketch. He stayed at the Lynam farm at Schooner Head, became enraptured with the scenery, and spread the word. Presently other members of the school, such as Thomas Birch, Frederick E. Church, Charles Dix and William Hart, came to paint and sketch. They stayed in Somesville at the Somes Tavern, in Bar Harbor with Tobias Roberts or Albert Higgins, in Southwest Harbor at Deacon Clark's, in Northeast Harbor with Squire Daniel Kimball or Augustus C. Savage. These were the vanguard who made Mount Desert known to the great world by their talk as well as their paintings.

A delightful summer's visit to Mount Desert in 1855 is recorded by Charles Tracy, a prominent New York lawyer, who was "sold" on the Island by Frederick Church. Mr. and Mrs. Tracy, with a bevy of children and a piano, landed at Southwest Harbor, spent a night at Deacon Clark's and proceeded to Abraham Somes's Tavern at Somesville, part by wagon, part by sailboat. They spent their days driving in a buckboard or walking. Everything they saw they raved over. The people were hospitable, and not unduly inquisitive like most Yankees; the Richardsons on Beech Hill showed the "utmost simplicity, kindness and contentment." The food — fresh milk and cream, berries, hot biscuits, fresh fish and meat, new peas and potatoes, pies and puddings — was excellent. Before leaving, the Tracys gave at the Somes Tavern a party of eighty people, all but a few of them permanent residents, whose young girls were pretty and showed "something of the practices and usages of society." A local fiddler and a flautist made a three-piece orchestra with the piano; they danced until 2 A.M. and served a supper of lobster salad, roast duck, sandwiches, custard, jellies and cake. The Tracy children were enraptured with the Island life, and one of them, who later became Mrs. J. Pierpont Morgan, was instrumental in bringing that eminent financier to Bar Harbor.

Even before the Civil War, the taverns began to be replaced by hotels, all built and run by local people. The war diverted the steamboats to government service and made it too difficult for summer visitors to reach the Island, but in 1865 the business of entertaining summer guests took a great spurt. By 1873 Stephen, Albert, Charles and Sam Higgins were each operating a hotel in Bar Harbor; and in 1887, when the big Colby-Stuart map of the Island came out, there were seventeen hotels there, one of which could take over five hundred guests, besides two at Seal Harbor, five at Northeast Harbor, six at Southwest Harbor, one at Sea Wall, two at Prettymarsh, one at Islesford and three at Somesville.

These hotels were not then, and never have become since, branches of hotel "chains" with drearily standardized food, furniture and misnamed "service." They were built and operated by a resident, who usually acted as his own manager, and whose wife often acted as *chef de cuisine*. The food, especially the fish, lobsters, pies and doughnuts, was all that a hungry small boy like myself could ask. (As I was not allowed to eat doughnuts, Mrs. Savage would make little round ones for me out of the same dough; they, having no holes, didn't count!) The waitresses were local girls, many of whom taught school in the winter until they were married. There was almost no tipping — a gift of ten dollars from one family to a waitress at the end of the season was considered generous. Many Mount Desert hotelkeepers were real "characters." Swift and Bush, who depicted the four Bar Harbor Higginses, have the proprietor of the Bayview Hotel telling three gentlemen who found their engaged rooms occupied:

> "There ain't no use, young men, you needn't shout;
> The folks is in and I can't git 'em out!"

Herman Savage of the Rock End would listen imperturbably to a guest's complaints, but always made the same reply: "One folk's board's good's another's!"

Cruising yachtsmen, too, had a part in spreading the news that Mount Desert Island offered the most spectacular scenery and the jolliest simple life of any place on the East Coast. Annals of yachting cruises Down East are few and rare before the 1880's, probably because of the difficulties of navigation. Except for the lighthouses we have mentioned, to which Bass Harbor Head was added in 1858, and the monument on East Bunkers Ledge and the three harbor buoys, there were no aids to navigation before the Civil War. Blount (1854 edition) advises masters of vessels bound up Blue Hill Bay to "take a pilot at Robertson's (Tinker's) Island, for it is not fit for a stranger to go without one." That is what yachtsmen did, if they were not so fortunate as to have a local sailing master who was "acquainted." Robert Carter in 1858 chartered sloop *Helen* at Swampscott for $7.50 a day, including wages of two local hands, but he had to take a pilot along the Maine coast. When Charles W. Eliot, the thirty-seven-year-old President of Harvard University, bought sloop *Jessie* in 1871 and made the first of many cruises in these waters, he exchanged salutes with seven vessels of the Eastern Yacht Club off Schooner Head, but there were still no good charts of these waters and few buoys. The first edition of the *Atlantic Coast Pilot* was just out, and Dr. Eliot was able to make many suggestions for its improvement. Next year he had sloop *Sunshine* built especially for Down East cruising, and visited Mount Desert waters every summer, camping for part of the time on Calf Island, Frenchmans Bay.

In 1875, however, the Federal Government began to

show great activity in buoying or otherwise marking Maine waters. The *List of Beacons, Buoys . . . and Other Day-Marks in the First Light-House District* for 1881 shows the approaches to Bar Harbor and to Mount Desert Harbor to be almost as well marked as today. For the former, you had Egg Rock light, buoys off Otter Cliff and Schooner Head, and more up the bay. For the Eastern Way approach to Mount Desert Harbor you had the two lights, the East Bunkers Ledge monument, buoys off Hardings and Bowdens Ledges, Lewis Rock and Long Pond Shoal. For the southward approach, up the Western Way, there was a buoy on The Drums, a spindle on South Bunkers Ledge, a bell buoy off Long Ledge, and three buoys for the narrow part of the channel. For Bass Harbor there was the light on the Head, two buoys marking Weavers Ledge, and one on Harbor Point Ledge. Ship and Barges had a spindle, Flye Island had the small lighthouse which was discontinued in 1935, and the main route thence to Ellsworth was also well marked.[1]

By the mid-1880's we have photographs of Bar Harbor filled with big handsome sailing and steam yachts from Boston, Newport and New York. Ample buoyage, publication of detailed charts, as well as the prospect of meeting pretty girls and being well entertained at Bar Harbor, made all the difference in the world to yachtsmen. Nevertheless, yachting here remained something of an adventure owing to the fre-

---

[1] It will be obvious to those who sail or fish these waters that, except for fairway buoys and an occasional whistler, little has been added since 1881. It seems strange that the successive government bureaus which take charge of day-marks have never buoyed the treacherous bar off Placentia Island, or the outlying rock in Bartlett Narrows, or the Lobster Rocks off Folly Island, which the charts persist in placing three feet under low water although they are visible except at a few neaps.

quent fogs that concealed the buoys, and the calms that were apt to leave any boat that did not reach a snug anchorage by 5 P.M., rolling miserably off shore all night. Nowadays any fool with a radar and a fathometer-equipped power boat can roar through the thoroughfares and passages, blow high blow low, fog or sunshine, as easily as he can drive a car.

Archaeologists digging up Mount Desert ten thousand years hence may well decide that there were at least four layers here of summer-visitor culture, corresponding to the three of the Indians. First came artists and scientists who camped or boarded around; then simple families of clergymen, college professors and the like, largely from Bangor and Boston, who took hotel rooms and wanted nothing of the Island but what they found, taking their pleasure in boating, fishing, walking, driving in buckboards and picnicking. Then came people of wealth and taste from all the Eastern cities, who built big "cottages," demanded and obtained water supply and electricity, tennis courts, golf courses, yacht races and swimming pools. They also founded clubs, such as the Bar Harbor Reading Room where, under the Maine prohibition law, most of the "reading" was done through the bottom of a glass. Your archaeologist of A.D. 12,000 may be puzzled by evidence that some of the old and simple families, like cliff-dwellers of the Southwest, managed to survive the millionaire invasion and cling to Mount Desert, if only by emigrating to the "back side" where the simple old mores continued. The penultimate "layer" consists of multimillionaires who, fleeing from life's complications in a palace on Bellevue Avenue, Newport, erected equally sumptuous palaces on the shore between Bar Harbor and Salisbury Cove. This has been aptly named by one of the earlier rusticators the "Stotesbury–Widener–Atwater Kent era," which ended abruptly with the great Bar Harbor fire of 1947. Most of the palaces not already given to charitable organizations were then consumed. This led to the final era, that of the motel and the Acadia National Park camp and trailer grounds, which has had the effect of sprinkling many of our beauty spots with empty beer cans, broken bottles and other trash. Archaeologists of the future will certainly make strange inferences on the state of American culture in 1960! Northeast and Seal Harbors, however, have set their faces sternly against motels and the like.

Many families who came first as "boarders" later bought land and became "cottagers," and in due course many of the cottagers, who came here for rest, found the summer social whirl so exhausting that they had to build "camps" on the Blue Hill Bay side to recuperate from life in the "cottage."

It should be explained for the benefit of posterity that on Mount Desert a permanent resident's house is a *house;* but a summer resident's house is either a *camp* if very simple, with no interior sheathing or plastering; otherwise it is a *cottage*, no matter how elaborate. Many years ago I heard the news "Edsel Ford is building a million-dollar cottage at Seal Harbor."

Bar Harbor acquired a *kudos* that the other resorts could not match from a visit of the North Atlantic Squadron, U.S. Navy, in September 1882, accompanied by Secretary of the Navy William E. Chandler and President Chester A. Arthur. These visits, always the occasion for much entertaining on board and ashore, were repeated almost annually. Occasionally the other Island harbors were favored by the smaller warships. A coaling station for the Navy was built at East Lamoine in 1902 but given up after a few years' operation.

In 1900, and again almost annually from 1920, Bar Harbor was visited by ships of the Royal Navy, and occasionally by the French Navy. The Italian cruiser *Raimondo Montecuccoli* anchored off Northeast Harbor on 22 August 1958 and entertained many members of the summer colony very pleasantly. Extensive maneuvers were held by the North Atlantic Squadron from Bar Harbor as a base in 1903.

Of the Northeast Harbor summer colony, the founders were three great but very dissimilar men: the Right Reverend William Croswell Doane, Bishop of Albany; Charles W. Eliot, LL.D., President of Harvard University; and Joseph H. Curtis, landscape architect. The Bishop first boarded with Squire Daniel Kimball at the site of the present Kimball House in 1880; then bought land and had built for him opposite the hotel, in 1881, the house punningly named *Magnum Donum*. Shortly after, his son-in-law James T. Gardiner and his fellow Albanian, Erastus Corning, purchased Sargent Head. Also in 1881 — it was a matter of friendly debate who came first — President Eliot built his cottage at the eastern entrance to the harbor, as he had been recommended to do by his son Charles Eliot, the landscape architect. Young Eliot had already camped at the head of the harbor, near Augustus C. Savage's "Harbor Cottages," which became the Asticou Inn.

It is not generally known that President Eliot's first choice for a summer residence was Calf Island off Sorrento in Frenchmans Bay, where he and his sons had camped for parts of several summers in the intervals of their yachting cruises. It so happened that when "Prexy" attempted to buy Calf Island, Sorrento was in the midst of a spurious gold rush. A couple of jokers, who claimed that they had found "pay dirt" on the Waukeag Peninsula, organized a gold mining company, and sold stock to the credulous, near and far. When Eliot, uninterested in these golden prospects, made a good offer for Calf Island, the owner, learning that he had been a chemist by profession, jumped to the conclusion that the President had found gold on the island, and refused to sell. Dr. Eliot then took his son's advice and visited Northeast Harbor. After being offered Sargent Head, and refusing it as too full of stumps, he worked around the harbor, and bought 120 acres, some of which his grandchildren still own, on the shore behind Bear Island.

Joseph H. Curtis in 1880 bought most of the eastern shore of Northeast Harbor adjoining Dr. Eliot's, gave it the name Asticou, and lived there every summer of his life. He laid out "Asticou Terraces," stretching up the hill of that name to "Thuya Lodge," and by will established the Curtis Trust to maintain the Terraces, thus becoming one of the leading benefactors of the Island, in a class with John D. Rockefeller, Jr., Robert Abbe, George B. Dorr — and your Uncle Sugar.

When the first summer people came to Northeast Harbor there was only one store and about a dozen houses, but no church. With money given by Mrs. Edward Perkins, Bishop Doane built the first wooden chapel, named St. Marys-by-the-Sea, in 1882; it was replaced twenty years later by a stone church. President Eliot, not to be outdone by an Episcopalian, helped raise the money which in 1889 built the Union Church, which some local wit promptly christened "St. Charles-in-the-Woods." Some bulls-eye glass windows were installed in the Union Church, and Captain Jonah Corson got a reputation for irreverence by calling them "the devil's spy-glasses."

Any pleasant afternoon in summer, over a period of thirty years, Bishop Doane could be seen wearing a dark blue Norfolk jacket and a rakish gray felt hat with *Only* printed in gold letters on the hatband, either pulling an oar or at the tiller of his six-oar rowing barge thus named.[2] The bow oar was always pulled by Nathan Fenelly, the gardener-care-taker, and the others by more or less reluctant guests and grandchildren. One day in a fog, Fenelly saw that the *Only* was being steered directly for Gilpatrick's Ledge, and sang out. The Bishop said, somewhat petulantly, "Fenelly, I have been cognizant of these waters for thirty years and know my way." "Well, Bishop," retorted Fenelly, "if you don't change course to starboard you'll learn more in the next thirty seconds than you did in the last thirty years!" The Bishop changed course.

At this point I wish to remark that the anecdotes of Bishop Doane and President Eliot "fawning" on J. Pierpont Morgan, in Cleveland Amory's book *The Last Resorts,* are, like most of Amory's yarns, both apocryphal and mislead-ing. Eliot paid little or no attention to Morgan, but the Bishop and the financier were good friends. That was natu-ral enough, Morgan being a leading layman and benefactor of the Episcopal Church and Bishop Doane a prominent cler-gyman, a wonderful preacher as well as good all-round man. At the turn of the century, Morgan spent a part of every summer at Bar Harbor on board his steam yacht *Corsair,* or at the cottage of his daughter Mrs. Satterlee. If he heard that Bishop Doane was to preach at St. Mary's-by-the-Sea, he would get up a party to steam to Northeast Harbor on the yacht. She left Bar Harbor promptly at 9:00, when a hearty breakfast was served in the dining saloon. Off Great

[2] As there was some local resentment over this name, owing to a mistaken notion that the Bishop claimed some sort of exclusiveness for his rowboat, I wish to record that *Only* was the family nickname for Daisy Doane, the daughter who died in the early eighties, and the boat was named after her.

Head, where the ocean swell comes in, the *Corsair* would begin to roll, the conversation to languish, and the faces of the ladies to grow pale, until Mr. Morgan said, "Don't wait for me!" and a dignified exit began toward the companion-way and fresh air.

On one of these occasions, when Bishop Doane had been notified to expect the Morgan party at morning service, the yacht was slightly delayed. Mrs. Doane, a fidgety little lady, became very nervous and peered out from *Magnum Donum* porch in the hope of seeing some sign of the yacht's approach. Suddenly she saw smoke and cried out, "She's coming! She's coming!" Fenelly, who was doing Sabbatical chores nearby, was heard to mutter, "Old fool! Don't know difference 'twixt smoke of *Mount Desert* coming in Western Way and smoke of *Corsair* coming in Eastern Way!"

The Southwest Harbor summer colony began in 1882 with cottages built by W. P. Dickey, presumably of Philadelphia, and A. B. Farnham of Bangor. But Southwest Harbor was slow to expand as a summer resort, because the fish industry there was going strong, and most rusticators were too delicate to appreciate the odors of the lobster canning factory at Clarks Point and the fish wharves at Manset. Nowadays we think that these things add a pleasant tang to the wind. Southwest Harbor's "cottages" were to a great extent made-over houses of permanent residents.

It used to be said that to be a summer resident at Bar Harbor you needed money but no brains; at Northeast Harbor you wanted brains but no money; but at Southwest Harbor, neither brains nor money! One can guess where that story started, but it is a gross libel on Southwest Harbor, which attracted college presidents and professors after the other resorts had become too expensive for them.

In the meantime Seal Harbor developed as a summer resort through the enterprise of the Jordans and the Clements in building hotels and selling land to the "right people." Nor were the Northeast Harbor landowners deficient in that delicate art. One of the stories I heard in my youth is Captain Gilpatrick's reply to the agent of a prominent though not very reputable financier, who offered to buy his entire farm for an attractive figure. The Captain insisted on knowing who wanted it, and the agent told him. "We have some very fine people here now in Northeast Harbor," said he, "including a bishop and three college presidents. We don't want any Wall Street riffraff!" And that was that.

A similar story was told about Bar Harbor after it had become a favorite summer resort for diplomats. The wife of the envoy extraordinary and minister plenipotentiary from Imperial Russia to the United States expressed a desire to purchase a certain tract of land. The owner inquired who she might be. "I am the wife of the Russian Minister," she said. "We have many good ministers here," he replied, "but we don't want a Russian one!" And that deal, too, was never consummated.

These "fine people" at Northeast, however, once got their comeuppance from Clem Walls, the village halfwit. He was sitting in Arthur Gilpatrick's store when Bishop Doane and Presidents Eliot of Harvard, Low of Columbia, and Gilman of Johns Hopkins dropped in to make some purchases and joined the circle around the cracker barrel. Arthur Gilpatrick, a great wag, turned to the halfwit and said, "Clem, can you tell who's the biggest fool in this store?" Clem looked around solemnly from face to face, and replied, "Hard to tell."

One of the characteristics of the Mount Desert people, as distinct from inland Yankees, was their sense of rank and dignity. Justices of the peace were addressed as "Squire," deacons of the Congregational churches as "Deacon," masters of vessels as "Captain," and elderly widows who had grown-up children as "Madam." My friends the Lorings were once entertained in a fishing camp with a wonderful fish chowder, made in a black iron kettle that had "never been washed, only scraped out," by two old bachelors. The guests were puzzled because only one of their hosts sat at table with them while the other ate in the kitchen. It was explained that he was "part Injun, had no right to eat with quality." Summer visitors were always addressed as Mr. and Mrs., or by their titles of Doctor, Reverend, Commodore, and so on, and were expected to reply in the same way in return. By exception, children were always called by their first names, with no Miss or Master attached; and if these children made good in the permanent community, they continued to be addressed by their elders and contemporaries with their first names all their lives. I dare say that the "Rockefeller boys" are still called David and Nelson in Seal Harbor.

The later years of the summer colonies, beginning with the admission of motor vehicles and the organization of the Acadia National Park in 1916–1917, and the story of the Great Fire of 1947, I do not intend to relate here, since this recent part of our history is very well told in Richard W. Hale's *Story of Bar Harbor*.

9. Yachting

YACHT racing has been a feature of the summer season in Mount Desert waters since the early 1890's. Bar Harbor, around 1900, had Nat Herreshoff design and build a dozen or more gaff-headed sloops called the "Bar Harbor Thirties." They measured 31 feet 6 inches on the waterline, 49 feet over all, 10 feet 5 inches beam, drew 7 feet 6 inches and had a large sail plan. These raced regularly for only a few years, and gradually were sold elsewhere, but they made excellent cruisers. Two of them, rerigged Marconi, visited our waters in 1959. Before World War I, Bar Harbor had a 17½ waterline class, and after the war it started a class of about 15 feet waterline, called the "M.D.I." These, too, languished; Bar Harbor's tastes in amusements have never been strongly aquatic.

Northeast Harbor, however, has become the principal yachting center on the Atlantic Coast east of Marblehead. Here there have been informal races since the 1880's, but the first organized class was the 21-foot knockabout. The first two, *Nordica* and *Gaviota*, were brought in by the Fraziers in 1897. They raced with Dr. Peabody's *Opeechee*, S. W. Colton Jr.'s *Spider*, James Roosevelt's *Dabster*, and another, whose name I have forgotten, sailed by the Reverend Tertius van Dyke of Seal Harbor. There was also competition between a few North Haven dinghies owned by Doane Gardiner, Sam Vaughan, the Thorp girls of

Greenings Island, and myself. Around 1902 Northeast Harbor had a 21-raceabout class, of which Francis W. Grant's *Pirate* was the champion, and with which others raced on a handicap basis. Among these were Dr. George Hayward's *Chief*, Ted Madeira's first *Sagamore*, my racing scow *Vampire* and 22-footer *Mariposa*, Robert and Huntington Williams's 22-footer *Satana*. Of all this fleet only the 14-foot dinghy *Bob* is still afloat, now being sailed by the grandchildren of Mrs. Robert Winthrop Knowles, who was Amy Thorp.

A new era began in 1914 when Northeast Harbor summer residents purchased from Dark Harbor six one-design 17-foot waterline gaff-headed sloops, which had been built by Lawley in 1910 from a design by Edwin A. Boardman. These proved so successful that more were acquired, and some of these were still being raced as "A" Class in 1959. This must be the oldest one-design racing class in the country except the North Haven dinghies. Class "B" of 17-footers, slightly smaller than "A," was added in 1921. The local yacht owners, among whom Charles D. Dickey, Jr. and George Davenport Hayward were leaders, organized the Northeast Harbor Fleet as a yacht club in 1923. That year the "O" Class of 15-footers was added to the yachting program, in 1925 the "M.D.I.," and in 1929 the "30-Squares" from Sweden. The annual three-day August cruise to ports in Blue Hill Bay started in 1922. That still goes on, but the "B," the "O," the "M.D.I." and the "30-Squares" have been given up as racing classes.

The most important addition to the Northeast Harbor fleet was the acquisition of fourteen cutters of the International class, built by Bjarne Aas of Fredrikstad, Norway, in 1938. At that time James G. Ducey, who had become the leading spirit of the fleet, persuaded it to set up a system of sailing instruction and seamanship for young children. This was necessary to keep yacht racing going, as the older generation of professional sailors, bred to the sea, who taught my generation, was passing away. It was his initiative that established the 16-foot Luders class in 1946, and the Herreshoff 12-foot Bullseys and 12-foot plexiglass Mercurys in which younger children matriculate as yachtsmen. These four classes, as well as the "A," have survived World War II and inflation; and the Northeast Harbor Fleet has purchased the old Rock End dock and established a clubhouse on the shore of Gilpatricks Cove. Southwest Harbor has its own plexiglass 12-footers. At Somesville, around 1935, Donald Gilpin built up two classes — the Massachusetts Bay catboats known as "Huskies," and the "Brutal Beasts."

With some forty cruising yachts in the Northeast Harbor Fleet, and E. Farnham Butler building "Controversy" reversed-sheer yachts at his Somesville yard, two building and repair yards at Southwest Harbor (Hinckley's and Southwest Boat Corporation), and George Bunker building seagoing power boats, yachting at Mount Desert Island is in a very healthy condition.

Mount Desert has never taken to power boats, generally referred to scathingly as "stink-pots" by the real yachtsmen, and their owners as "monkey-wrench sailors." But most people who live on the Cranberries, Suttons and other islands found that they had to have a power boat to get about. The earliest were small steamers; then came a rash of naphtha launches (steamers using high-test gasoline, then called naphtha, as fuel), conspicuous by having the engine in the stern, surmounted by a tall brass funnel. President Low's *Surprise*, named after the famous clipper ship owned by his forebears, was one that lasted many years. The first boat powered by an internal combustion engine was brought in by a Mr. Bolland in 1897. She seldom traveled more than twenty feet without stalling; but the Hoar boys, Sam and Jack, had one in 1901, named *Concord* after their native village, which really proved herself. About that time the owners of Friendship sloops began installing one-cylinder Knox gasoline engines, built at Camden, Maine, and no longer had to mount topmasts and bend on gaff-topsails to catch the lightest whiff of air.

10. The Steamboats

A ND now a few words about the steamboats, which pre-
ceded the rusticators, and flourished with the develop-
ment of the summer resorts, but were killed by motor car
competition some twenty-five years ago. Regular runs to
Southwest and Bar Harbors from Rockland and Portland
began in the 1850's. I first came to Mount Desert in 1890 on
board the *City of Richmond*, which had been built as a trans-
port in the Civil War. She was owned by her skipper, Captain Charles Deering, who carried no insurance and in a thick
fog was wont to anchor, while his competitors felt their
way along by listening to sheep blatting on the rocky islands,
or by the echoes of their own steam whistles. On one occasion when the *City of Richmond* had anchored for a long
time, a passenger inquired of Captain Deering, "Aren't you
going on?" "Nope." "Why not? It's all clear overhead."
"We're not bound that way!" The *City of Richmond* called
regularly only at Southwest and Bar Harbors, but she made
one memorable stop at Northeast Harbor, right up against
the ledge where the steamboat wharf was later built, because Mrs. Adelma Joy was on board with her summer supply of dry goods and notions, and charmed Captain Deering
into setting her and her goods ashore on the rocks.

The classically named *Ulysses*, first to ply regularly the
Rockland–Bar Harbor route, sank in 1878 but was shortly
replaced by the *Mount Desert*. "Old Mounty" and her air-

less main cabin upholstered in plush, which had absorbed plenty of upsets and subtly invited others, is one of my earliest memories. She enjoyed a quarter-century of active life on that route until replaced by the *J. T. Morse* in 1904. All our nineteenth-century steamers were side-wheelers, with walking-beam engines, and they were not ashamed of being side-wheelers; their paddle boxes displayed glorious sunbursts in red and gold leaf, sometimes with paintings of scenery, Indians or the Maine coat of arms at the hub. Steamers on this run had to be side-wheelers so that they could slip over Bass Harbor Bar and the two shoal spots in the Western Way at low tide, but the later ones concealed their paddle boxes by sheathing so that they looked like screw steamers.

Captains and other officers came and went; but the trusty permanent officer of the Rockland–Bar Harbor line was stewardess Maggie Higgins. Serving first in the *Ulysses*, she catered to *Mount Desert* passengers during its entire life and then transferred to the *J. T. Morse*, where she continued twenty summers more, until pensioned off at the age of eighty after half a century of devoted service. Maggie was the first to greet us when we came on board the *Mount Desert* or the *Morse* at Rockland at 4 or 5 A.M, feeling groggy after a night on the Bangor boat. She got us a place at the breakfast table; or if we were so lucky as to have a stateroom, brought us breakfast in bed. She doctored the seasick and amused the children; she exchanged sage remarks on Republican politics with V.I.P. passengers. She knew all the "regulars" by name and followed the careers of their children and grandchildren. In her latter years on the *Morse* she called the landings in her old cracked voice — "No'theast Ha'bor — landin' on the lower deck for'd!" because the seamen's union wouldn't allow the colored porter to do it. Blessed be Maggie Higgins! At sight of her in July the delights of summer began; and when we said good-by to her at the Rockland wharf in September, the grown-up world of school and college closed around us.

Then there were the fast Maine Central Railroad Steamers, connecting with trains at Hancock Point. The exotically named *Sappho,* suggestive of Lesbos rather than our Island, was succeeded by the *Pemaquid, Norumbega, Moosehead* and *Rangeley,* which at one time made three round trips a day between the railhead in Hancock, and Manset. These were the aristocrats of the Maine steamboat world — efficient, fast and brass-bound. If one took the night train from Boston or New York to Mount Desert Ferry, one looked forward to the delicious breakfast of coffee, scrambled eggs and hashed brown potatoes on board the "ferry boat."

Little *Cimbria,* named after the Russian cruiser, plied between Bangor and Bar Harbor, calling at all the Eggemoggin Reach ports and at Bass Harbor, as well as Southwest, Northeast and Seal Harbors. The majestic *Frank Jones,* which succeeded *City of Richmond* on the Portland-Machiasport run, was too big to touch at Seal Harbor, but made all the other whistle stops, and you could hear her paddles chunking through the Western Way before her hoarse whistle blew for Southwest Harbor.[1] *Golden Rod* plied between Mount Desert Island harbors only. She was the favorite steamer for day excursions to Bar Harbor; but she was a bad roller and off Great Head many of the expensive dinners eaten at Sproul's restaurant, and ice-cream sodas imbibed at

[1] *Frank Jones* was patronized, among others, by lumberjacks of the Machias River region, for whose benefit there was a notice in each stateroom: "Gentlemen will please remove their boots before going to bed."

Bee's, were lost before the passengers reached home. Then there was little *Islesford*, owned and mastered by Captain Hadlock, whose long white beard, when he stuck his head out of the tiny pilothouse, almost swept the deck. She did the same job as the Islesford ferry of today; but occasionally when the tide was right she made an excursion all around Mount Desert Island at a dollar a head. Captain Hadlock was adept at the witty retort. On one of these round-the-island excursions, *Islesford* called at Lamoine, and the skipper announced that she would stay there an hour. "What in the world is there to do here?" said my mother. "Take off your shoes and stockings and run around in a potato patch!" was the reply.

In the descending scale of steam-driven craft I must mention the *Bismarck*, a steam launch built, owned, mastered and engineered by Captain Keene of Southwest Harbor, who always referred to her as "The Steamer." He was highly insulted when Sam Vaughan and I, after pooling our financial resources at the age of fourteen, proposed to charter her for a deep-sea fishing party in honor of the fascinating Georgiana Farr. Smallest of all were steam launches which plied no regular schedule but were on charter for picnic parties. One referred to them as the "teakettles," since their boilers took up about half the available space. There were the *Silver Crest* and *S.V.R. Hunter* at Northeast Harbor, and the more imposing *Creedmoor* and *Mascot* at Bar Harbor. Around the turn of the century most summer residents chartered a Friendship sloop, whose owner used her for fishing and lobstering in the winter, but mounted a topmast and bent on a gaff-topsail for summer "plesurin'." Having no engines, the Friendships were very apt to be becalmed late in the afternoon. That was when the "teakettles" made their killing. They sallied forth and took becalmed sloops with hungry passengers in tow, at five dollars a boat; and it was not uncommon to see *S.V.R. Hunter* puffing home with four or five Friendships and other yachts in tow.

All this came to an end with the internal combustion engine, which successively put out of business the schooner, the steamboat, the horse and the livery stable. Many were the summer visitors, and permanent residents too, who cried "Mount Desert is ruined." And there are very disquieting things in the present situation — rowdy motor tourists who throw trash about, and the ruthless ambition of the Maine Highway Commission to make speedways out of beautiful winding roads. But we who love this Island say that it can never be ruined while the tide ebbs and flows twice a day and an offshore wind turns the sea to an incredible blue, or the east wind brings wreaths of fog that clothe the coasts and hills in soft white. It can never be ruined while the Acadia National Park keeps up the trails; while the Northeast Harbor Fleet continues its good work of indoctrinating the rising generation in the arts of oar and sail; while members of the old stock are here to greet us every summer, not with compliments, but with honest appraisals of how "peakéd" we look after winter in the city. Mount Desert is not merely an island; it is a way of life to which one becomes addicted; and if we are permitted in the hereafter to enter that abode where the just are made perfect, let us hope that it may have some resemblance to Champlain's *Isle des Monts Déserts*.

APPENDIX I

Bibliography

I. PRINTED BOOKS, PAMPHLETS AND ARTICLES

JOSEPH ALLEN, JR. *The Steamer* J. T. Morse, *Her History and Adventures*. Reprinted from *Old-Time New England*. Portland: The Southworth-Athoensen Press, 1937.

FREDERICK S. ALLIS, JR. (ed.). *William Bingham's Maine Lands, 1790–1820*. Colonial Society of Massachusetts *Publications*, Vols. XXXVI and XXXVII (1954).
Documents from the Baring, Bingham, Cobb and Knox Mss. with an Introduction, containing an immense amount of valuable information on the settlement of Mount Desert Island and the adjacent mainland. Many old maps and portraits. The Baring account quoted in my text is in XXXVII, 765–800.

The Bar Harbor Times includes in its files many interesting historical articles, notably Miss La Rue Spiker's "Story of a Century and a Half of Seal Harbor," August 20, 1959.

PIERRE BIARD. *Relation* of the Saint Sauveur colony. Reprinted with translation in R. G. Thwaites (ed.) *Jesuit Relations* III and IV (Cleveland: The Burrows Brothers Company, 1897).
The translation only is reprinted, together with Argall's account, from *Purchase His Pilgrims*, in Charles H. Levermore (ed.) *Forerunners and Competitors of the Pilgrims and Puritans*. Brooklyn: The New England Society (1912), Vol. II.

EVA L. BUTLER & WENDELL S. HADLOCK. *Uses of Birch Bark in the Northeast.* Robert Abbe Museum of Bar Harbor Bulletin VII (1957).

Comprehensive and well illustrated.

ROBERT CARTER. *A Summer Cruise on the Coast of New England.* Boston: Crosby and Nichols, 1864; second edition, Boston: Cupples and Hurd, 1888.

The earliest account of a yachting cruise to Mount Desert.

SAMUEL DE CHAMPLAIN. *Works,* H. H. Langton & W. F. Ganong (eds.). Toronto: The Champlain Society, 1922.

Vol. I, reprinting Champlain's *Des Sauvages,* contains his account of the discovery of Mount Desert, text and translation, with ample notes. The Portfolio of Plates and Maps added to this edition has the best reproduction of Champlain's Ms. Map of 1607 (original in the Library of Congress) showing "I. des Monts déserts."

SIGMUND DIAMOND. "Norumbega: New England Xanadu." *American Neptune* XII (1951), 95–107.

B. F. DeCOSTA. *Rambles in Mount Desert.* New York: Randolph & Co., 1871.

Best of the early guidebooks, well illustrated with photographs.

FANNY H. ECKSTORM & M. W. SMITH (eds.). *The Minstrelsy of Maine.* Boston: Houghton Mifflin Co., 1937.

The best collection of Mount Desert ballads.

CHARLES W. ELIOT. *Charles Eliot, Landscape Architect.* Boston: Houghton Mifflin Co., 1903.

CHARLES W. ELIOT. *John Gilley, Maine Farmer and Fisherman.* Boston: American Unitarian Association, 1904.

This little classic first appeared in an article, "Forgotten Millions: John Gilley" in *The Century Magazine* LIX (November

(899), 120–130. It has frequently been reprinted as a book, recently by the Idlewild Press, Cornwall-on-Hudson, 1947.

FRANCES H. ELIOT. "Patriarchal Picnics." *Atlantic Monthly* CXCII (July 1953), 55–60. Also "I Remember Mount Desert." *Lincoln-Mercury Times* (May–June 1951).

[SIR FERDINANDO GORGES.] *Briefe Relation of the Discovery and Plantation of New England.* London, 1622. Reprinted in J. P. Baxter *Sir Ferdinando Gorges and his Province of Maine* (Boston: Prince Society, 1890).

This is the only early publication that uses the name Mount Mansell for Mount Desert, and it tells about the Indians hunting moose.

WENDELL S. HADLOCK. "Bone Implements from Shell Heaps around Frenchman's Bay, Maine." *American Antiquity* VIII No. 4 (April 1943), reprinted by Robert Abbe Museum, Bar Harbor.

RICHARD W. HALE, JR. *The Story of Bar Harbor.* New York: Ives Washburn, Inc., 1949.

This sesquicentennial history includes the best account of the pre-settlement history of Mount Desert Island, and of the history of the last forty years, and includes a comprehensive bibliography.

MAINE HISTORICAL RECORDS SURVEY. *Inventory of Town and City Archives of Maine,* No. 5, Hancock Co., Vol. I, *Towns of Mount Desert.* Mimeographed book published by the Survey. Portland: 1938.

S. E. MORISON. "The Course of the *Arbella* from Cape Sable to Salem." Colonial Society of Massachusetts *Publications* XXVIII (1930), 285–306.

Reproduces Winthrop's and later English *Coast Pilot* profiles of the mountains.

S. E. Morison (ed.). "A French Description of Frenchman's Bay, 1792." *New England Quarterly* I (1928), 396–410.

The account by Bancel de Confoulens (whose name, owing to his undecipherable signature, I misspelled Congoulin).

The Northeast Harbor Fleet. Annual handbook for 1954, containing an historical sketch of yacht racing there.

Leonard Opdycke. *Naval Visits to Bar Harbor.* Bar Harbor: The Bar Harbor Times Publishing Co., 1952.

Captain William Owen. "Narrative of American Voyages and Travels . . . 1766–1771." In New York Public Library *Bulletin* XXXV (1931) 71–98, 139–162, 263–300, 659–685, 705–755.

Well edited, with copious notes, by Victor H. Paltsits.

Francis Parkman. *Pioneers of France in the New World.* Boston: Little, Brown & Co., 1865, and many later editions.

The chapters relating to the discovery of Mount Desert and Saint Sauveur are reprinted in S. E. Morison (ed.) *The Parkman Reader* (Boston: Little Brown and Company, 1955). The English ed., published by Faber & Faber, London, is called *England and France in North America.*

John M. Richardson. *Steamboat Lore of the Penobscot.* Augusta: Kennebec Journal Print Shop, 1941.

Lavishly illustrated and full of interesting anecdotes.

William Otis Sawtelle. "Sir Francis Bernard and his Grant of Mount Desert." Colonial Society of Massachusetts *Publications* XXIV (1923) 197–254.

Includes a reproduction of the rare Des Barres *Atlantic Neptune* chart of the Island and adjacent waters.

Nathaniel S. Shaler. *Autobiography.* Boston: Houghton Mifflin Company, 1909.

Chapter IX relates his cruise along the Maine Coast in 1860.

GEORGE A. STREET. *Mount Desert, a History,* edited by Samuel A. Eliot. Boston: Houghton Mifflin, 1905. New edition, revised by the editor, 1926.

The standard history of the island.

[HENRY WALTON SWIFT AND DACRE BUSH]. *Mount Desert in 1873, Portrayed in Crayon and Quill.* Boston: J. R. Osgood (1874).

An amusing illustrated account of the Bar Harbor summer colony.

[TALLEYRAND-PÉRIGORD, C. M.]. *Talleyrand's Unpublished Letters and Memoirs,* translated and edited by H. Huth and W. J. Pugh in American Historical Association *Annual Report* for 1941, Vol. II. Washington: Government Printing Office, 1942.

MRS. SETH S. THORNTON. *Traditions and Records of Southwest Harbor and Somesville.* Privately printed, 1938.

An immense amount of data nowhere else to be found.

[WILLIAM W. VAUGHAN]. *Northeast Harbor Reminiscences, by an Old Summer Resident.* Hallowell, Maine: White & Horn Co., 1930.

2. MANUSCRIPTS

GOVERNOR FRANCIS BERNARD's Official Papers Vol. X. Sparks Mss. Harvard College Library.

Contains his "Journal of a Voyage to the Island of Mount desart."

ABRAM GILPATRICK. "Reminiscences of Northeast Harbor," 1929.

Basis of the Vaughan item above, with much additional data. Property of his daughter, Mrs. Julia Manchester. Copy in Northeast Harbor Library.

MANUSCRIPT COLLECTIONS OF THE JESUP LIBRARY, BAR HARBOR, AND OF THE ISLESFORD AND MOUNT DESERT MUSEUMS.

The Jesup has a typescript copy of Charles Tracy's "Log of a Voyage from New York to Mount Desert and return, July–September 1855," genealogies of leading Island families, and Eben M. Hamor's typed copies from the Mount Desert and Eden Town Records.

NATIONAL ARCHIVES, WASHINGTON, D.C. Records of the Coast and Geodetic Survey.

Invaluable for data on establishing lighthouses, buoys, etc.

NORTHEAST HARBOR WOMEN'S CLUB. Copies of historical papers in the custody of Mrs. Stella Hill, Northeast Harbor.

Especially useful are Adelma F. Joy "Reminiscences of Somesville," Stella Hill "Echoes of Long Ago," Augustus C. Savage "Memories of a Lifetime," Mary Wheelwright "Reminiscences of Yachting," and Emma F. Spurling "Lighthouses of Mount Desert."

MRS. HAROLD PEABODY (née Marian Lawrence, daughter of the Bishop of Massachusetts), "Old Bar Harbor Days." In her possession.

3. MAPS AND CHARTS
(Arranged Chronologically)

DIEGO RIBERO MAP of 1629. Best reproduction in Edward L. Stevenson *Maps Illustrating Early Discovery and Exploration in America 1502–1530, Reproduced by Photography from the Original Manuscripts.* New Brunswick; N. J.: 1903. Of the many maps derived from it the clearest is in Alonso de Santa Cruz *Isolario* (1560), reproduced in Henry Harrisse *Discovery of North America* (Paris and London, 1892).

"A Plan of the Islands Eastward laying from Penobscot Bay & of the Granted Townships, with their Distances and Bearings from each Other and from the Continent (which is bordered and shaded with Green), agreable to a Resolve of the Great and General Court for the Province of the Massachusetts Bay . . . per John Jones & Barnabas Mason, Surveyors, February 13 1765." Ms. in Massachusetts Archives; photostat in Northeast Harbor Library.

A remarkably accurate outline map of Mount Desert and neighboring islands, in some respects better than the one that follows. Shows the first road on the island, from Somesville to Northeast Arm.

SAMUEL HOLLAND. "Chart of the Maine Coast, 1772." Photostat in the Islesford Museum. So far as Mount Desert is concerned, this map is reproduced in every detail in the sumptuous album by J. F. W. Des Barres called *The Atlantic Neptune*, published in London between 1777 and 1784. No two copies of this album are alike. See article in New York Public Library *Bulletin* XL 571 (July, 1936).

SALEM TOWN. "Survey of the Bernard half of the Island, 1896." Ms. in Mount Desert Historical Society's Museum, Somesville.

JOHN & JAMES PETERS. "Survey of the De Grégoire half of the Island, 1807." Ms. in the collection of the Bar Harbor Historical Society, Jesup Library, Bar Harbor. A modern reproduction of it has been made, and is on sale in Bar Harbor book stores.

These two surveys give the owners of every lot.

CAPTAIN SEWARD PORTER. "Chart of the Coast of Maine," 1837, Part No. 4. Copy in Harvard College Library.

The first general map of Maine following *The Atlantic Neptune* to depict the Island in any detail.

JOHN S. DODGE. "Survey of Southern Mount Desert, 1848." Ms. in Northeast Harbor Library.

Shows ownership of each lot.

H. F. WALLING. *Topographical Map of Hancock Co.* New York: Lee & Marsh, 1860.

Wall size; weak on topography, but shows many houses with names of owners.

U. S. COAST AND GEODETIC SURVEY Engraved Chart No. 292, *Mount Desert Island*, first edition, 1875, gives the coast in greater detail than any subsequent chart, and has full details of the land, indicating wooded and cleared areas, roads, boundaries of lots, and every house. A reduced copy, simplified, was printed with Loring, Short & Harmon *Illustrated Guide Book for Mount Desert Island*, 1877 and 1879 editions.

The above was the basis for Coast Chart No. 103, *Mount Desert Island, Frenchman's and Blue Hill Bays and Approaches*, Scale 1/80,000, first issued in May, 1883. This is the first chart showing soundings, buoys and monuments. It continued to be reissued with hydrographic corrections until about 1910, when it was superseded by the simplified charts of *Eastern Mount Desert & Frenchmans Bay*, and *Western Mount Desert and Blue Hill Bay*.

COLBY & STUART. Large, colored, wall-size "Map of Mount Desert Island," 1887.

A blown-up version of the chart as far as land data is concerned, but adds all buildings, and the names of landowners. Copy in Northeast Harbor Library. A reduced version of it was published for F. D. Foster, Bar Harbor, the same year.

EDWARD L. RAND and JOHN H. REDFIELD. *The Flora of Mount Desert Island, Maine*. Cambridge: John Wilson, 1894. Includes a map which corrects and adds to the nomenclature of the U. S. Coast and Geodetic Survey chart, and was later republished separately.

The above is the basis for U. S. Dept. of the Interior Geological Survey *Topographic Map Acadia National Park and Vicinity*, first published in 1942, and frequently republished. This has the new George B. Dorr names of the mountains.

Nomenclature

I. THE MOUNTAINS

Apparently it did not occur to anyone to name the hills of Mount Desert before summer visitors came. Only two (Westward and Bauld) are found on maps before 1860; Charles Tracy, an inveterate inquirer of place names, in 1855 got only four, and the Hancock County map of 1860 has only four. But all are named in B. F. DeCosta *Rambles in Mount Desert* (New York: 1871), and all are on the government chart of 1875 and the Colby & Stuart map of 1887. After the Acadia National Park was created most of these names were changed; and this has led to great confusion, as many signs carrying the old names remain to this day (1960) while others bearing the new names have been erected. So here I am giving the old names, which the older residents still use, and the official National Park names of today, with explanations.

Old names — if more than one is given, the last is that found on the 1875 chart	*New names — official Acadia National Park*
Newport (Christopher Newport, captain of the Jamestown fleet, 1607)	Champlain (the discoverer)
Round Peak, Picket	Huguenot Head (one of Mr. Dorr's fancies)
Dry (having no springs) [1]	Flying Squadron (of U.S.N.), later renamed Dorr (for George B.)

[1] On the 1860 Hancock Co. map Dry Mountain is called Kebo, the name of the hill from which the Bar Harbor Golf Club takes its name; but this was probably an error. Origin of name "Kebo" is a mystery.

Old names — if more than one is given, the last is that found on the 1875 chart	New names — official Acadia National Park
Bauld (Peters 1807), Newport (Tracy 1855), Green (having many springs)	Cadillac (the bogus Sieur de)
Black, Pemetic (the Indian name of the island, meaning range of mountains)	unchanged
Sargent (Tracy 1855; a family who owned land north of it)	unchanged
The Bubbles (euphemism for "Bubbies")	unchanged
Jordan (the adjacent pond)	Penobscot
Brown's (John Brown owned the 117-acre lot just north of it)	Norumbega (fabled city on the Penobscot)
Little Brown's	Parkman (the historian)
Asticou (the Sagamore), or Savage's Hill	Eliot (Charles W.)
Robinson (family who lived in the valley)	Acadia (French name for this region)
Dog (Tracy says because a dog fell over the cliff)	St. Sauveur (for nearby Saint-Sauveur, French colony)
Flying (Tracy was told of an Indian tradition that this was a piece of Dog Mountain that flew off and landed in the Sound)	unchanged
Beech	unchanged
Westward (Town 1807), Western	unchanged
East Peak, Western	Mansell (Sir Robert)
West Peak, Western	Bernard (Sir Francis)

II. OTHER NAMES

Most Island names are either connected with an early owner (see the list of early settlers in the Street *History*) or with birds and animals that frequented the place (Duck, Goose, Bear, Moose, Otter, Seal etc.). But some names require explanation, and others have changed with changes of ownership. When the Tracys visited the Island in 1855, many of the ponds had no names; and "Young's Pond" and "Denning's Pond" were re-named Eagle Lake and Echo Lake by early tourists.

Starting at the Narrows and working around to the East and South, we have the following:

Eden: The name of Bar Harbor township from 1796 to 1918. When the people of this part of Mount Desert petitioned the General Court for a separate township in 1796 they asked to be named Adams after Governor Samuel Adams. But there was already an Adams township in Berkshire County, and when the bill went to the Governor, in February, 1796, the new town was named Eden, evidently for the Garden of. Alexander Baring, after sailing to Mount Desert that very summer of 1796, states in the long letter he wrote about it, in December 1796, "that part of Mount Desert is incorporated into a town by the name of Eden, which the inhabitants gave it in consequence of its fertility."

Salisbury (or Salsbury) Cove: Ebenezer Salsbury from Nova Scotia, one of the earliest settlers at Bar Harbor, who later located at the Cove.

Point Levi: Levi Higgins, an early settler, who owned the land.

The Porcupines: From their resemblance to those animals. Sheep Porcupine was originally "She Porcupine."

Ironbound Island: From its cliffy southern coast. An iron-bound coast means a rocky shoreline without beaches or coves.

Stave Island: Barrel staves were formerly made there.

Sol's Cliff or Sallis Cliff: Solomon Higgins, son of Dean Higgins who lived nearby.

Thrumcap: Thrums are rope yarns, which old-time sailors used to weave into skull caps for themselves. Hence any round, bare island was called a thrumcap. The little island at the entrance to Seal Harbor was also given this name before it became wooded. The spellings Thumbcap and Thrumbcap are incorrect.

Schooner Head: The white marks on the southern face, which at a distance resemble a schooner's sails. A British warship is said to have fired on it during the War of Independence when, approached through a fog, it failed to answer a hail!

Northeast Harbor: Both because it is the northeasterly branch of the Great Harbor, and a refuge from the northeast wind.

Southwest Harbor: So called by Governor Bernard in 1762. See Northeast.

Cranberry Islands: So called by Governor Bernard in 1762, obviously from the cranberry bogs.

Deadmans Point, Great Cranberry: A corpse was washed up there more than a century ago.

Maypole Point, Little Cranberry Island: According to a story related by Rachel Field in *Calico Bush* (1931), Marguerite, the little French "bound-out" girl of Joel Sargent's family, erected a maypole here to divert the Indians.

Islesford: Properly the name of the village and post office, not of the island.

Bakers Island: So called in *The Atlantic Neptune* chart of 1774; but who Baker was, everyone has forgotten.

Suttons Island: Ebenezer Sutton bought it in 1755. He sold it to a man named Lancaster, and it was sometimes called Lancaster's Island, but reverted to the name Sutton.

Greenings Island: The third owner, who inhabited the old house on the southwest point in 1860. Called *Langley's Island* on the 1848 survey, and *Somes's Island* in the Holland survey of 1772 and the Peters survey of 1807.

Norwoods Cove: Even Mrs. Thornton doesn't know who Norwood was.

Somes Sound: From Abraham Somes, the first settler. Prior to that it was called "Mount Desert River."

Manset: Some clerk's mistake for Mansell (Sir Robert), the early English grantee.

South Bunkers Ledge: The real name is "Bunker's Whore." The story goes that a certain Captain Bunker took the town trollop of Southwest Harbor sailing in his sloop, and that they "carried on" so that the vessel ran hard and fast on this ledge.

Gotts, or *Great Gotts Island:* From Daniel Gott, an early settler at Bass Harbor, who bought the two Gott Islands in 1789 and moved to the larger one. *Cross Island* on one of the charts in *The Atlantic Neptune,* and *Little Placentia* on another, as well as on the 1837 Chart of the Maine Coast. This is evidently the equivalent of *Petit Pleasure,* where Governor Andros reported that two families were settled in 1688. Captain Owen calls it *Tom's Island* in the narrative of his cruise in 1770.

Placentia Island: Thus in Owen's narrative; *Great Placentia* in *The Atlantic Neptune*. Conjecturally, at some time in the seventeenth century a Frenchman settled there and called it his *Plaisance*. The local pronunciation, "Placench," is nearer to this French word than to "Placentia." Stories that Champlain named it *Plaisance* are not supported by his writings or his maps.

Black Island: Thus in *The Atlantic Neptune*. This was a common name for islands covered with a heavy growth of spruce.

Ship Harbor: A local vessel, pursued by an English man of war, ran in during the War of Independence at high water, grounding so hard and fast that she never got off. Called *Locust Reach* in the government chart of 1875, for no apparent reason.

Bass Harbor: Thus in *The Atlantic Neptune*. The name probably goes back to the seventeenth century, when striped bass was the most esteemed food fish in New England, and was caught by nets set out in harbors.

Swans Island: Its proprietor, James Swan, was an eighteenth-century land speculator. *Burnt Coat Island* in *The Atlantic Neptune*, a name preserved for the principal harbor. Probably derived from its having been burned over.

Black, Opechee and *Pond Islands*, on the north side of Casco Passage, are respectively *Grass, Charles* and *Pond* on the Holland chart of 1772. *Pond* becomes *Pound* in *The Atlantic Neptune*, doubtless a mistake, as there is a pond on the island.

Lamp Island: From its resemblance to an old-fashioned whale-oil lamp.

Ship Island, and *Ship and Barges Ledge:* When Ship Island had a few trees on it, if viewed from the eastward it resembled an old-time high-pooped ship being towed in a calm by her rowing barges.

Tinkers Island: "Robinson's" in Owen's *Narrative* of 1770, "Robison's" in *The Atlantic Neptune*, and "Robertson's Island" in Blount's *American Coast Pilot* (1854). Tinker bought it for a keg of rum from Robinson or Robertson, who used to go about Seal Cove complaining of the poor bargain he had made.

Seal Cove: Still a resort for seals. *Bay of Gulls* in the Holland chart and *The Atlantic Neptune*.

Hardwood Island has a beautiful grove of ancient beech trees on its northern half. *Beech Island* in *The Atlantic Neptune*.

Sawyers Cove, originally *Billings:* Its eastern arm was called by old inhabitants *Phantom Cove* because a full rigged phantom ship would be seen sailing out of it whenever any sailor from the neighborhood was lost at sea. The western arm was called *Spirits' Cove* because the ghosts of drowned sailors congregated there. The ledge off its mouth is called *Merriman's Ledge*, from the master of a vessel that hit it over a century ago.

The Cape, on the Rand map of 1894, is the name of an old school district that ran from near Center to Seal Cove. The real name of the promontory on the west side of Sawyers Cove is *Stewarts Cape*, from the owners, and the next cove south is *Jinny's Cove*, from the wife of an old settler.

Center, the village that strings along the main road from near Prettymarsh Harbor almost to Seal Cove, was so called because it was once the center of religious interest on the west side of Mount Desert. The Congregational or Baptist meeting house at the cross roads, deserted since early in the present century, was built as early as 1820.

Folly Island: So called over a century ago because two claimants went to law over it, and the judge pronounced that it was "folly" to contend for so small an island.

Bartletts Island: The earliest settler, Christopher Bartlett, who landed there about 1762. *Hog Island* in *The Atlantic Neptune*.

Alley Point, the southwestern point of Bartletts Island: Captain Alley lived there after his retirement. Folks said that he had been a pirate, that he buried a pot of gold in the woods behind his home, and that when he died his body was laid out in the uniform of a British naval officer whom he had forced to walk the plank!

Dogfish Cove, Bartletts Island, as shown on modern maps and charts is misplaced; it is the tiny cove in the southernmost headland of Bartletts. The proper name for the one now called Dogfish Cove is *Old Field Cove*, from the abandoned field at the head of it. The Rand map of 1894 is the only one that has it correctly.

Brig Landing Cove, called *Brig Cove* on the 1894 map: This is the one with the little island just north of Alley Point. The name is explained in my text.

Black Island off High Head: Probably not, like other Black

Islands, so called from a dense growth of spruce, but from a hermit who lived there early in the last century. He used to make his few purchases at Somesville (which he visited once or twice a year) with golden guineas which he was supposed to have fished up from the wreck of a British warship in the channel.

Indian Point has reference to the big Indian shell-heap in this neighborhood.

Thompson Island: From Colonel Cornelius Thompson, who came to Mount Desert from Salem before the Revolution, in which he was a colonel of militia and skipper of privateer brig *Chase.* Colonel Thompson's grandson was an officer in the Civil War, and after its close brought home with him one or more families of emancipated Negroes. That is why the drawbridge in the old wooden bridge over the Narrows used to be raised by colored men. Presumably *Negro Point* was where one of these settled.